"This book teaches important tac
    oping strategy for *Smart Nego*
principles in my business as we
really impresses me is the easiness in understanding Dolan's
tactics and strategies. I really got a lot out of this book and
will use it as a guide in negotiations that I have coming up."

—JIM TUNNEY, ED.D., FORMER NFL REFEREE,

"John Patrick                                                    stin-
guished on m                                                    *)eal!*
he does what                                                    forward and ea                                                     : of
the art. Joh                                                    ll

DISCARD

—TERF

"*Smart Nego*                                                   tant
    classic.  It's                                             :k
Dolan's keer                                                   and
    the profes                                                 "

—ROGER

"There a
synonym
Dolan IS                                                       :
with the
    bool

**Date Due**

—LARRY WINGE     BRODART, CO.          Cat. No. 23-233-003     Printed in U.S.A.     HOST
OF A&E TELEVISION'S *BIG SPENDER*

"John Patrick Dolan's done it again. The man never ceases to amaze me with his depth of insight and understanding. Reading his latest book, *Smart Negotiating: It's a Done Deal*, captivated me for hours as I read and reread each page and chapter . . . . absorbing the powerful subliminal psychologies Dolan presents as he reveals the secrets of influence and negotiation. This book is power-reading for power-people."

—James A. Ziegler, CSP, HSG, President, Ziegler Dynamics, Inc., and Author of *The Prosperity Equation*

"The book is engaging, entertaining and offers practical solutions to everyday situations from home to office! Easy and fun to read . . . Not at all what some may expect from a great legal mind!"

—Janita Cooper, CEO, Master Duplicating Corporation

"Everybody has a price. Very few get it. The difference between the price you want to sell for and the price you end up with is determined by your negotiating skills. This book is not only an eye-opener; it's a wallet-opener. Cost of this book: $19.95. Ability to get the price you are asking for: Priceless."

—Jeffrey Gitomer, Author of *The Little Red Book of Selling* and *The Little Red Book of Sales Answers*

"*Smart Negotiating* is essential reading if you want to create the best future for yourself, and your organization."

—Daniel Burrus, Author of *Technotrends*

# SMART
# NEGOTIATING

# SMART NEGOTIATING

## It's a Done Deal

### John Patrick Dolan

EP
Entrepreneur.
Press

Editorial director: Jere L. Calmes
Cover design: Pay Fan
Composition and production: Eliot House Productions

This publication is designed to provide accurate and authoritative information in regard to the subject matter covered. It is sold with the understanding
that the publisher is not engaged in rendering legal, accounting, or other professional services. If legal advice or other expert assistance is required, the
services of a competent professional person should be sought.

**Library of Congress Cataloging-in-Publication Data**
    Dolan, John Patrick, 1949–
       Smart negotiating: it's a done deal/by John Patrick Dolan.
         p.    cm.
       ISBN 1-59918-003-0 (9781599180038: alk. paper)
       1. Negotiation. I. Title.
    BF637.N4D635 2006
    302.3—dc22                      2005029827

Printed in Canada

11 10 09 08 07 06                    10 9 8 7 6 5 4 3 2 1

# Table
# of Contents

# Foreword

Over the past 15 years I have read over 3,000 books on success covering just about every area of life and business. I know hundreds of business writers personally. I currently read approximately 100 business books per year. Most of them are crap. They are written by well meaning, well educated, well-informed people who have some degree of familiarity with their subject. Some are even written by experts in their field of writing. After reading as many books as I have, I've discovered that just reading the words of an expert isn't good enough for me any longer. I find myself wanting more. After all, if you take the time to climb the mountain in order to learn, you want to do it at the feet of a master. Not at the feet of a mere expert and not at the feet of just a smart person.

There is an old saying that goes something like: "Do what the masters do and you too will become a master."

Great saying. Great idea. One problem. There are very few masters. There are a lot of experts. There are many who know a lot. But there are few masters.

A master is someone who goes beyond knowledge and expertise to become their topic. They don't just know their material. They *are* their material.

Who they are becomes synonymous with what they talk about. From the stage to real life, from the written word to the streets, there is no difference in how they think, speak, or act.

Based on that definition, how many masters do you know? Again, I know of only a few. John Patrick Dolan is one of the few.

In my world, the world of professional speaking and writing, John Patrick Dolan's name is synonymous with negotiations. He is known as *the* speaker on the subject, because he *is* the subject.

In his real life he lives, eats, and breathes negotiations. As a renowned trial lawyer, he relies on these skills daily. As a consultant to some of the world's leading corporations and associations he is acclaimed for his ability to communicate the essence of negotiations in a way that can be duplicated in business and life.

Past that, there are other reasons why I would go to Dolan and this book to do the job. Most business books are full of jargon, charts, graphs, and studies that don't tell you a thing about how to get the job done. Some books are so intellectual that you can't comprehend their meaning. Their stories are so ridiculous that no one can picture himself in that situation. *Smart Negotiating* isn't like that. It's not full of words you won't understand or situations you can't relate to. Dolan talks like the rest of us. He uses stories that we can all identify with. He goes beyond the skills and techniques of negotiations and gets at the heart and essence of why it is a part of our daily life and all we do.

He will get you thinking about not only the science and strategy of how to negotiate but about the philosophy behind the art of negotiating. After reading this book and applying the concepts within, your life and business will change for the better because you will know what to do to achieve the results you want. That is the real test: The ability to apply in every day situations what you have learned in order to achieve the results you want.

Don't look any farther than *Smart Negotiating* or John Patrick Dolan to learn how to negotiate because you have arrived at the feet of a master.

—Larry Winget, author of
*Shut Up, Stop Whining & Get A Life!*
and host of A&E's *Big Spender*

# Preface

J. B. CLOSES HIS OFFICE DOOR, WALKS OVER, AND SITS BEHIND HIS desk. Looking at Bob, he says, "We closed on the Fiskins project yesterday, which presents our company with a tremendous opportunity. If we can prove ourselves on this job, I think we'll open the door to many more million-dollar contracts."

Bob says, "That's great, J.B. What's the next step?"

"The next step," J.B. says, "is to get to work right away. This project isn't going to be a cinch. It's going to be an all-hands-on-deck endeavor."

"I see," Bob responds.

"We're counting on you to lead the team since you're one of our top managers," J.B. continues. "I believe you can rally the kind of spirit and commitment it's going to take to finish the project on time and at a high-quality level. People are going to have to work long and hard hours. Do you think you can handle it?"

"You know I'm a team player, J.B., and I want to do what's good for the company," Bob answers, "but I have to tell you; I'm swamped right now. And from what I know about the Fiskins project, it is going to take a lot of overtime and hard work. I don't see how I can do a top-notch job on that project and handle all the regular accounts I manage. I don't think you're aware of how much I have to do already."

J.B. responds, "Well, I don't want our regular accounts to slide, but this Fiskins project does take priority. Will it help if we shift some of your accounts to other people in the department? Hasn't Margaret done some work with you on the Jones account? Do you think she can manage it for a while? And what about the Johnson and Filbert accounts? Do you think someone else could handle that while you focus on the Fiskins project?"

"Probably," Bob says. "It would take some time to bring people up to date on my accounts, but I think that would work out OK. The smaller accounts I manage are really no big deal. Just about anybody could maintain them for a while."

J.B. asks, "Do you think it's possible for you to transfer your accounts to these other people by the weekend? That way, you can start on Fiskins first thing Monday."

"If everyone is willing and can make time this week, I don't see a problem with that," Bob answers.

*That's negotiation!*

Elaine, an office employee, walks up to the secretary's desk on Monday morning and says, "Barbara, do we have any refill cartridges for the computer printer?"

Barbara says, "Did you look in the supply closet?"

Elaine answers, "I didn't see any refills for the hallway printer. If we don't have any, it would probably be a good idea to order a couple. We have several projects that will be wrapped up in the next week or so, and I don't think the cartridge we're using now will hold up."

Barbara responds, "To tell you the truth, Elaine, I don't see how I'm going to have time in the next couple of days to take care of that. The boss just gave me a week's worth of dictation he needs to be typed up and mailed out by tomorrow afternoon, plus all the end-of-quarter reports are due by Friday. Do we really need a refill in the next couple of days?"

Elaine says, "Yes, we do, or we stand a chance of missing some important deadlines. Will it help any if I find the refill number for you so you don't have to take the time to look it up?"

"That'll make it a whole lot easier," Barbara responds. "Just put the number on my desk next to the phone, and I'll place the order either this afternoon or first thing tomorrow morning. Will that be soon enough?"

Elaine says, "Sure," and goes to get the cartridge number.

*That's negotiation!*

James comes through the front door, hangs his coat over the back of a living room chair, tosses his briefcase beside it, and heads into the bedroom to change clothes. His wife, Melissa, meets him as he's coming down the hall. "Jim, the Carmichaels are coming over for dinner tonight. I really need your help in the kitchen."

"I was planning to mow the lawn," Jim responds.

Melissa says, "James, the Carmichaels will be here in an hour and a half. If you mow the lawn now, not only will dinner not be ready when they arrive; you'll probably be in the shower."

Jim says, "It's supposed to start raining tomorrow. If I don't mow the lawn this afternoon, it might be another week before I'll have a chance. And you know how shaggy it looks already."

"I know the yard isn't going to win any awards," Melissa says, "but it can wait; dinner can't. I don't want Jan and Gary waiting an hour for dinner because you're still working in the yard. Help me with dinner tonight, and get to the yard this weekend. It'll still be there."

"The yard will still be there, but I was planning on hitting some tennis on Saturday," Jim says.

"I tell you what," Melissa proposes. "If you'll help me in the kitchen tonight, I'll help you in the yard Saturday. I'll do the weeding. You know how you hate that job."

"OK," Jim says. "Where do you want to start with dinner?"

*That's negotiation!*

Any human activity that involves two or more persons usually requires some degree of negotiation. Asking for help at work, coordinating chores at home, discussing give-and-take arrangements on the job: most of us deal with these kinds of situations several times a week. In fact, it's about as easy to avoid negotiating as it is to avoid breathing. Unfortunately, negotiating effectively, unlike breathing, is not an automatic reflex for most of us.

Even though we spend a great deal of our time negotiating for things we want, most of us are not natural-born negotiators. We may be afraid to ask for what we want, so we go without. Or we ask for too little or demand too much. Basically, a lot of people just don't know how to get what they want without being forceful or rude.

## • You Can Learn to Negotiate Effectively

If you understand the process of exactly what it means to negotiate effectively, you can improve your performance at the bargaining table immensely. If you are committed to getting what you want in life, you can become an expert negotiator by mastering the basic strategies and tactics that work in all kinds of negotiations, from convincing your spouse to help with the housework, to hammering out an acceptable compensation package with your boss, to buying a house, to just about anything.

As a trial lawyer, I've handled everything from simple wills to death-penalty murder cases. As a consultant who provides training and development programs for businesses and legal professionals, I spend many hours working out the details of consulting packages and fees with my clients. In other words, the bargaining table is a second home to me. And, although every case is a unique negotiating opportunity, most of the strategies and tactics I share in *Smart Negotiating* can be modified to suit any occasion.

## • Is This Book for You?

Have you ever walked away from negotiations shaking your head and saying to yourself, "Boy, is she a shrewd negotiator. I just gave up everything but my first-born child."

Have you ever felt like you could have negotiated a better deal if only you had known what you were getting into?

Have you ever wished you were the kind of person who would "drive a hard bargain"?

If you answered "yes" to any of those questions, this book is for you. Most people don't consider themselves "negotiators." They believe negotiating is reserved for the big-league players in business and politics. Well, wipe that misconception out of your mind. That myth is one of many that this book blows out of the water. Negotiating is unavoidable if you ever have contact with other people. And it can be a fun and rewarding experience if you know what you're doing.

Read *Smart Negotiating*, and you'll know what you're doing. This book, which is based on years of experience and the study of many expert negotiators, is a comprehensive guide to effective negotiation. In it, you will discover the pragmatic strategies and tactics that translate into power at the bargaining table. You will also learn about the dynamics of the negotiating process, which will help you build on your strengths as a negotiator.

By the time you finish reading *Smart Negotiating*, you will have the power to get what you ask for.

# CHAPTER ONE

# The Dolan Strategy for Effective Negotiation

NEGOTIATION IS ONE OF THE MOST COMMONLY PRACTICED FUNC-tions of communication; yet it is one of the least understood arts of human interchange. Most of us don't think of our-selves as negotiators, certainly not as professional negotia-tors. When we think of professional negotiators, we visualize hard-charging corporate raiders who launch attacks on businesses, or diplomats meeting to determine the fates of nations, or lawyers settling million-dollar lawsuits.

As discussed in the introduction, negotiation takes a wide variety of forms. Most of us are negotiating all day. If you and your spouse are deciding who's going to pre-pare dinner and who's going to clean up the dirty dishes, you're negotiating. Or if you're a salesperson attempting to close a deal with a prospect, you're also negotiating. Any time you work out any kind of agreement with anyone, you're negotiating. That goes for heavy negotiations as well.

For instance, most of us will buy or sell a car, a home, or some other major item at least once every few years. Those negotiations have serious implications for the quality of our lives. Say you're able to negotiate the price of a home down 15 percent from the asking price. By the time you add points and interest on a 20-year mortgage, it's realistic to expect to save a year's salary over the life of the loan.

What about when you're negotiating for a new job? The terms you agree on will have a far-reaching impact, not only with that company but possibly the rest of your career. For most of us, the compensation package we draw at one company will set the pattern for the level of income we can command when negotiating with another employer. It's not unusual for the difference between the earnings of two individuals to have far less to do with skills and talents than it does with each person's ability to negotiate.

Because most people don't understand the dynamics of negotiating, they are frightened by the prospect of sitting down at the bargaining table. They get sweaty palms and nervous stomachs when they face the prospect of haggling over the price of a car or working out the terms of an employment contract. The trouble is, they believe all the myths and legends surrounding this vital activity.

## • Getting Past the Myths of Negotiation

Do you believe that only jerks and ruthless people are good negotiators?

Do you picture negotiations as people facing each other from opposite sides of a table, with each group trying to beat the other out of a good deal?

If you answered "yes" to either of those questions, you have inaccurate perceptions of effective negotiating. And those false perceptions are probably preventing you from negotiating like a pro.

Effective negotiating has a great deal to do with attitude. If you approach negotiating as a win-or-lose battle, you'll struggle against the people you're negotiating with. You'll waste a lot of time and energy defending positions and trying to sneak something past your negotiating counterparts. When all is said and done, you will likely end up with less than if you had treated the negotiation as an opportunity for everyone involved to profit.

Here are several mythbusters that can improve your attitude toward negotiating:

**Mythbuster 1.** You don't have to be a jerk to be a good negotiator. In fact, most jerks got to be that way because they were lousy negotiators and had to resort to ruthlessness to get what they wanted.

**Mythbuster 2.** Negotiating is not synonymous with fighting. Fighting only breaks out when people cannot negotiate effectively.

**Mythbuster 3.** Negotiating effectively is not a talent reserved only for a shrewd business person, an experienced diplomat, or a precocious child. Anyone can learn to negotiate effectively. It doesn't require manipulation or an IQ of 200.

**Mythbuster 4.** You don't have to abandon all your ethics to get what you want at the bargaining table. Getting what you want doesn't mean stealing it from others.

**Mythbuster 5.** You don't have to have the upper hand to negotiate effectively. Actually, the weaker your position, the better you must negotiate.

**Mythbuster 6.** Negotiating is not a time-wasting activity that clogs up the wheels of progress. Done right, it is an enormous timesaver because it gets everybody working together.

**Mythbuster 7.** Negotiating is not always a formal process with clearly defined parameters and procedures. It is the sum and substance of all human give and take.

Because we all have to negotiate constantly, it's vital to get beyond the myths and legends that accelerate our pulse rates and cause us to ask for less than we want or deserve. The people who overcome the fallacies of negotiation are able to reap rich benefits.

- They can make and save more money.
- They can get more of whatever they want and forge better, more productive relationships in all areas of life.
- They can head off many misunderstandings and conflicts, and amicably settle those that do arise.
- They can enlist the aid of others who can help them fulfill their dreams and plans.
- They can avoid being conned into doing things they don't want to do.
- They can mediate conflicts, misunderstandings, and stale-mates between other people and groups.
- They can become more professional and effective in the way they deal with all types of people.

Learning to negotiate can produce all these positive effects because negotiating is more than trading off with others for the things you want. Rather, it is understanding people and discovering ways to work together to produce positive results for everyone involved.

### • What Is Effective Negotiation?

Now that you know what is *not* effective negotiation, I'm sure you want to know what *is* effective negotiation. In one sentence, effective negotiation is: *Working side-by-side with another party (or parties) to achieve mutually beneficial and satisfactory results.* No, it's not a fancy definition and you don't need a law dictionary to understand any word in it. But don't let the simplicity of that statement mislead you. Its implications are profound.

Think about it: Negotiating is working side-by-side with another party or parties to achieve mutually beneficial results. Is that how you envision the proceedings when you have to negotiate with others? Probably not. But open your mind and you will discover an approach to negotiating that will give you the power to open doors for you.

How effectively you negotiate depends on how well you understand two basic concepts.

## • *Concept 1*

To negotiate effectively, you must be able to read people and relate to them.

The concept of working side-by-side with another party (or parties) is foreign to many negotiating situations, but I consider it a key element of negotiating. Negotiations occur between people, not between companies, agencies, unions, dealerships, associations, or other organizations. No matter what you're negotiating, no matter what agencies or organizations are being represented at the bargaining table, when it comes down to it, you are negotiating with people, with individuals. I cringe when I read in the paper about negotiations breaking down between management and a union, or between countries. Negotiations don't break down between institutions; they break down between people. To be a good negotiator, you cannot overlook the "people" element.

This means that when you sit down across the table from the person you're negotiating with, you see that person as an individual like yourself. You recognize that he or she has feelings, desires, and fears, and you accept that, just like you, that person wants something from your negotiations. Otherwise, you wouldn't be meeting.

Former Secretary of State Henry Kissinger tells a story about a visit he made to the late Chairman Mao Tse-tung. The famous Chinese leader asked Kissinger flatly, "What do you want from us?" Kissinger responded in diplomatic fashion: "We don't want anything but your friendship." Chairman Mao shot back, "If you want nothing, you shouldn't be here; and, if I wanted nothing, I wouldn't have invited you here."

It's not unusual for negotiations to break down because the people on either side of the bargaining table get so caught up in the issues that they forget they're dealing with human beings. They lose sight of the fears, feelings, and desires other people bring with them to negotiations. All they can see is their own position, and they start to view others involved in the negotiations as obstacles, maybe even enemies. No matter what's happening at the bargaining table, the real pros at negotiating always focus on the people involved, because then they can go beyond positions. When you focus on people, you build a sense of trust among the people involved in the negotiation. You can start to talk about what they really want and the most effective way to respond to their needs. That is the core of effective negotiation.

I tell the participants in my seminars, "If you aspire to become a master negotiator, develop strong interpersonal skills." In other words:

**Learn to read people.** Reading people is a critical part of my job as a lawyer. If you're defending someone on a murder charge, you want to know if that individual is being straight with you about all the facts. Over the years, I've learned to watch people, to monitor their words and actions, to look inside them through their eyes, and to hear and see what they're not telling me.

Being able to identify a person's real personality by studying the face he or she presents to the public is a valuable skill in negotiating. When you understand what motivates that person, you can predict his or her reactions to your words and actions.

Emerson wrote:

> *A man passes for what he's worth. What he is engraves itself on his face, on his form, on his fortunes, in letter of light. Concealment avails him nothing, boasting nothing.*

In other words, people can't keep their real selves hidden forever. Observe the individuals facing you from the other side of the issues, and you will learn a great deal about them and their negotiation style. Listen to their words, and listen for their meanings. This is an effective method for discovering what your negotiating counterparts really want.

**Develop double vision.** Try to understand the people you're negotiating with on their level. Ask yourself, "What do the negotiations look like from their perspective?" Expert negotiators seek to understand all dimensions of an issue.

Labor negotiations give us the best example of the damage that can result when one group fails to consider both sides of an issue. One of the most notorious cases involved the newspaper industry in New York City. Using weapons like crippling strikes and work stoppages, a printers' union insisted on and won what seemed like an ideal contract. Observers hailed Bertram Powers, who was head of the printers' union, as a negotiating wizard.

Unfortunately, the demands the newspapers were forced to accept precipitated their demise. One of the deadliest stipulations in the contract restricted newspapers from implementing certain technological advances that were vital to remaining competitive. That misguided effort to protect workers' jobs ultimately resulted in the closing of three of the city's newspapers. With only one evening and two morning papers operating, thousands of people in the newspaper industry—and not just printers— were out of work. Focusing only on your own immediate payoff can have dire consequences, so learn to consider negotiations from everyone's perspective.

**Get to know the people with whom you're negotiating.** Before you dive into negotiations, learn what you can about the other party as individuals. Try talking to them about yourself to break the ice, then ask them questions. What do they do? What circumstances led them into the negotiating situation? What are their aspirations? You might even be able to determine how these negotiations will affect their goals. The kinds of questions you can ask the people you're negotiating with vary according to negotiating situations.

**Draw a distinction between people and their positions.** You may not like the stance someone has taken, but that doesn't mean you have to attack that person. For example, let's say you're negotiating for a position with a company, and your prospective employer quotes a salary figure far below what you would be willing to accept. Don't get angry. Don't say something like, "What kind of fool do you think you're talking to?" Instead, a more effective strategy would be to calmly educate the person on why you would be worth much more to the company.

**Keep all negotiations on a mature, adult-to-adult level.** Don't approach negotiation as an opportunity to annihilate the party facing you from the other side of the issues. Instead, consider negotiations as an opportunity for you and the other people involved to work together to profit and benefit from your dealings. Relating to the people you're negotiating with as mature adults is fundamental to working alongside others and forging satisfactory agreements.

To relate to others on this level, you will have to be open and honest about what you want. For example, if you're looking at a house for sale, don't hesitate to tell the seller, "I like your home. I would like to be able to work out a fair deal with you." However, you don't have to tell the seller that if you don't get that particular house, life just isn't worth living. Never want anything that badly. But if you do want something that badly, never let the other person know that's how you feel.

**Maintain a positive attitude toward the negotiations.** Expect negotiations to proceed amicably, ethically, and in a direction that is acceptable to everyone involved. Even if you sense someone is trying to manipulate you, maintain your standards. Now, that doesn't mean that you allow manipulators and hardballers to take advantage of you. But don't drop down to their level. You can maintain your integrity throughout negotiations, no matter what the people you're negotiating with do. I'll talk in more detail about how to do that later in this book.

The tone of the relationships you share with the people you negotiate with will have a tremendous impact on your negotiations. Whether you are parrying in a brief encounter with a salesperson or dickering with your boss over a raise, the quality of the rapport and communication you share with that person will affect the way you negotiate and the results you can expect.

Because negotiations occur only between people, effective negotiations grow from constructive relationships.

### • *Concept 2*

A critical element of any negotiation is the relative perceptions of value among the people involved in the process. You've probably heard the phrase "The seller may set the price, but it is ultimately the buyer who determines the value." In other words, a sale can take place only when the value to the buyer becomes greater than the price of the seller.

What does this mean in the negotiation process? Primarily, it means that the value of what you have to offer depends on the perceptions of the person you're negotiating with. Say you're trying to sell your house. Now, in your mind, one of the selling points of the house is its close proximity to the city's business district. You have only a 25-minute commute every morning and afternoon. A looker seems interested, but he tells you, "I like the size of the house, but I was really looking for something a little more secluded." The house's location has no value to the buyer, no matter how important it was to you as a resident. Remember that values are never objective. As with the person looking at the house, a person's needs, experiences, and tastes will determine the value he or she places on an item or term.

What does all this mean to you as a negotiator? Keep in mind that the most effective negotiators are those who best understand how to deal with the value perceptions of all the people involved. Recognize that the people you're negotiating with may not value the same things you do and they may reject your definition of value. Once you understand this, you can learn to determine the value perceptions of the people you're negotiating with and respond to those values.

The seller of the house, for example, could stress that although the house is not very secluded, it is on a 1.5-acre lot in an established neighborhood. Anyone living there won't have to worry about a developer buying up land around the house and building a shopping mall or industrial park in his or her back-yard.

Effective negotiators focus on creating value (and percep-tions of value) for both sides in the bargaining process. There you have it: the expanded version of the one-sentence definition of effective negotiation. The bottom line is, if you can get together with the people you're negotiating with and arrange agreements that meet everyone's needs as they perceive them, you are nego-tiating effectively.

Now that I've covered the concepts behind effective negotia-tion, it's time to move on to concrete strategies and techniques you can use to keep negotiations on a mature level and to work with others to forge mutually beneficial agreements.

## • The Dolan Strategy

To negotiate effectively, you must have a basic strategy, that is, a master plan or a systematic approach to handling all negotia-tions. It doesn't have to be complicated or cumbersome. It just needs to be a method that works for you. In fact, the simpler it is, the more effective it will be.

Over the years, I've developed what I call the Dolan Strategy. This strategy is based on my experiences as a lawyer and busi-nessman, and on my observation of other expert negotiators. The most important thing is that it works well for me. I share it with you because you can adapt it to your own style and person-ality, and get the same positive results I do.

My strategy follows a series of simple, logical steps, which I describe in the following section.

### • Step 1: Always Be Prepared

All effective negotiations begin before you get to the bargaining table. Don't just jump in without any research or forethought. The more you know, the more effectively you can negotiate.

### • Step 2: Set Objective Negotiating Standards before You Begin Bartering

Make sure all parties agree on objective standards before you begin. That is, lay the ground rules. Governmental or organizational laws impose some standards. For example, most banks won't grant a loan for buying a house until that house has been inspected and declared structurally sound. That's a standard that exists before negotiations even begin. But most negotiators can set their own standards to ensure that negotiations go smoothly.

### • Step 3: Work with, Not Against, the People You're Negotiating with to Develop Mutually Beneficial Solutions

Expert negotiators understand that good negotiating means that all parties leave the table feeling good about the agreement, and about each other. The only way to ensure this feel-good result is for everyone involved to look for mutually beneficial solutions. Approaching negotiations with this attitude disarms the other party. Most people only get defensive when they feel that you are out for blood. If they really believe you want to play fairly with them, they'll usually try to play fairly with you.

Some people won't share your high standards, but that doesn't mean that you should abandon your strategy of fair play. I always warn people that even though you don't approach negotiations as a battle, the person on the other side of the issue might. Be prepared for your counterparts to pull out some heavy-duty weapons. In Chapter 7, I'll discuss some common manipulation and intimidation tactics that show up in negotiations and how you can deflect them.

For now, it's important to accept that nothing your opponent does should make you abandon your own strategy. I like Abe

Lincoln's advice: "When you find yourself arguing with a fool, make sure he's not similarly occupied."

### • *Step 4: Finalize All Agreements*
Don't leave any details hanging. Once you've found a solution, finalize agreements, and make sure everyone understands what's expected.

### • *Step 5: Follow Through*
Once the solutions have been developed and the agreements signed or otherwise finalized, follow through on your end of the bargain. Do what you said you would do, when you said you would do it, and in the manner you said you would do it. If you committed yourself to making payments, make them on schedule. If you have agreed to deliver a specific product or service, make sure the other party receives it when he or she expected it and in the manner expected.

   If for some reason you can't follow through, contact the person you negotiated with to discuss alternative arrangements and make sure the people you negotiate with follow through on their end of the bargain. Don't be a chump. For everything you give, make sure you get something in return.

### • It's a Done Deal
Some say that a strategy dictates the tactics you will use. Others argue that tactics control your strategy. I have always used tactics as the tools for implementing my strategy. After all, a strategy is only as strong as the techniques and tactics you use to carry it out. Throughout this book, I'll arm you with certain tactics, which will enable you to achieve your objectives.

## One Last Thought . . .

## Negotiating with Style

### The Platinum Rule

We all know the golden rule: "Do unto others as you would have them do unto you." Dr. Tony Alessandra in his book, *The Platinum Rule* (Warner Books, 1996) says there is a better way: "Do unto others as they want to be done unto."

How does this relate to negotiation? Quite simply we negotiate with people or groups of people. As the personality styles of our counterparts vary, so must we vary our approaches to different people. We can review the wonderful information in Dr. Alessandra's book and make some decisions as to our particular approach with particular personalities.

Different people observe, interpret, and act on information differently. Here is a short summary of the four styles that Dr. Alessandra discusses in his book:

1. *Directors.* Football coaches, drill sergeants, and dictators best describe Directors. They are challenge-oriented, take-charge decision makers. Achievement and success are defined by overcoming obstacles and realizing accomplishments. Directors like to take action, accept challenges, achieve and accomplish, and have a fear of being "soft." The best way to negotiate with a director is to offer him a selection of several potential alternatives and a deadline. Let him choose. He will feel "in charge" and if you're careful in designing the potential alternatives you will get what you want.

2. *Socializer.* These are "people" people, such as PR directors, salespeople, actors, and speakers. Appreciation and recognition are what the socializer seeks. Time spent schmoozing is time

well spent. The Socializer wants to "shoot the breeze," have fun, make a favorable impression, and speak with an articulate style. The biggest fear is one of being disliked. She wants you to be a friend, to inquire about her, and appreciate her wit. If a Socializer likes you and perceives the feeling to be reciprocated, she will do business with you and make you a great deal.

3. *Relaters*. These are people who are friendly and reliable. Relaters are team players who exercise extreme patience in difficult times and work for the long-term gain. Relaters prefer tranquility and stability. They desire a stable work environment and like to sit or stay in one place. They want predictability and reliability in any important transaction. They do not like surprises, changes, or modifications without advance notice. To successfully negotiate with the Relater you need to emphasize your trustworthiness and the predictable, reliable nature of the transaction. Following the process to predictable, reliable results works best here.

4. *Thinkers*. Serious, analytical people with long-term goals best describes a Thinker. They ponder choices until they have all the information and analysis to make a proper, well thought-out decision. Thinkers are often fact oriented and take pride in being meticulous. They want to know how things work and want time to analyze and organize tasks. Their work is high quality, although sometimes they take longer to do it. They can be perceived as over critical and sometimes insensitive. Their biggest fear is being wrong. They would rather not make a decision than to make a poor or incorrect (irrational) decision.

How each style tends to operate and how to negotiate with each is critical to the overall success in negotiations.

Negotiating is a person-to-person process. Have fun the next time you negotiate by observing carefully the personality style cues exhibited by your counterpart(s). Being sensitive to personality orientation can really increase success, reduce friction, and lead to better agreements. Try it. You'll be negotiating with style!

· · · ·

# CHAPTER TWO

# Preparing to Implement Your Strategy

WHEN YOU ARE NEGOTIATING, WHAT THOUGHTS RUN THROUGH your mind? Do you think, "There's much more at stake here than me getting my way," or "What are the real issues here?" or "What arrangement will produce the best results for everyone involved?"

My guess would be those are not your main concerns. If you're like most people, when you roll up your sleeves to negotiate, your mind dwells on such crucial points as, "What's in it for me?" and "What can I do to ensure I get what I want?" and "How can I be sure so-and-so doesn't take advantage of me?" That's the human reaction to negotiating. The self-preservation instinct kicks in and negotiations can quickly degenerate to kill-or-be-killed encounters.

But negotiations don't have to be that way. As a matter of fact, if you want to negotiate effectively, control your search-and-destroy instincts when you approach the bargaining table. The only way people involved in negotiations can move beyond a counterproductive struggle over positions and superficial issues is to adopt a comprehensive view of the event. In other words, don't focus only on what you want and ways you can get it. Look at the big picture. Try to determine all the elements involved and all the ramifications of various options open to you.

Take a look at this example. A man approaches his boss about a raise. The issues on the surface are clear: The man wants a raise; the employer wants to contain operating costs. But delve a little deeper into the situation, and you see that the issues are not that simple.

The employee feels that his work has been exemplary. He's demonstrated commitment, and the quality of his work has earned praise from management. He feels that he deserves a merit increase. In addition to that, he hasn't had a raise in more than a year, and inflation has been steadily eating away at his paycheck. He's beginning to experience a financial squeeze.

The employer acknowledges that the man's work has been more than satisfactory, but the company is experiencing a slow-down in sales and production. The projected profit-loss figures for the year are grim. If management starts handing out raises, the company could suffer from a debilitating cash flow problem.

After an initial discussion, the two parties seem to be at a stalemate. The company cannot give the man a raise, but the man can't afford to keep working for the company if he doesn't get a raise. The employee is happy in his job, but if he has to, he will look for another job that will pay more. The employer, who believes the company's problems are temporary, doesn't want to lose a valuable employee, but he can't get blood from a turnip.

In this case, if the employer and the employee dig in at their positions, they will both lose. Even if the man gets the raise he wants, what good will that do him if it puts the company in a precarious financial position? A weak company offers little security. On the other hand, what if the company loses the employee? They are having enough trouble with production without cutting a good employee from their work force. Considering the cost of hiring and training a new person who might not be as productive, replacing the employee is not an attractive option.

If, however, the two men are able to loosen their grip on their individual positions, look at the overall picture, and work together to find solutions, they can both win. For instance, the employer could offer the employee a bonus for projects completed. That way, the employee would be paid in line with income the company receives, and, in effect, be getting a raise. At the same time, the company wouldn't be committed to a salary increase irrespective of economic conditions. Another option is to agree to review the situation in three months and reopen negotiations if the company has pulled out of its slump.

The options available to negotiators depend on the circumstances surrounding their situations. If you want to negotiate effectively, arranging the best deal possible for everyone, you must consider all the circumstances involved. This is crucial so that people can begin to focus on finding solutions, rather than winning their positions. A critical step for getting a comprehensive view of a negotiating event is to prepare in advance.

## • Be Prepared

Always walk into negotiations well armed with the right kinds of information. If you don't have time to prepare, don't negotiate! It's like going into a supermarket when you're hungry without a shopping list. Those displays of impulse items will drain you for a fortune every time. That's why retailers put them at strategic places throughout the store. They want to catch you off guard. If you don't have time to prepare your defense, chances are you'll respond impulsively.

That's a clever tactic many shrewd negotiators use. You know how it goes. You're talking with your boss about an insignificant or routine matter and suddenly she says, "Oh, by the way . . . how would you like to move to Podunk, Idaho, and take over our operation there?"

What do you say? "Duhhh . . . That sounds good to me."

Don't fall for it if somebody makes you an offer or asks you for something on the spur of the moment. Find a way to buy some time. I know that's not always easy to do. The boss may be under pressure to make a sudden appointment, and you could pass up a good opportunity. Or she might just be testing your corporate loyalty. In either case, your answer could have a big impact on your career.

How do you handle such a situation? Make a noncommittal show of interest to find out what's behind the remark. For instance, say something like: "That's an interesting possibility, tell me more about what you have in mind." That says you're willing to negotiate, but it doesn't commit you to anything except talking about it. If it turns out that she's serious about sending you to the boondocks, say, "When would you like to fill me in on the details so I can give you an intelligent answer?" That sends the message that you want to be cooperative, but that you don't plan to make an ill-considered decision. Once you set up a definite time to talk about the proposed move, find out everything you can about what such a move would mean for you—both short term and long term.

In other words, if you think it's to your advantage to explore an offer or a request, try to find a way to keep the door open without making any commitments. That's a key function of negotiating—keeping doors to good opportunities from slamming in your face, but doing it in a way that keeps you from making serious mistakes. It takes a lot of tact and diplomacy, but it pays big dividends.

## • Passing the Preliminaries

The negotiating process begins long before two or more people actually sit down across from each other at the bargaining table. Smart negotiators realize that negotiating effectively depends on being prepared. Of course, how much preparation you do depends on what you're negotiating. Negotiating with a roommate over who's going to clean the bathroom and who's going to dust and vacuum obviously won't take as much preparation as negotiating the acquisition of a business. The strategies I share with you in this chapter can be used in the most sophisticated negotiations. You can, however, adapt them to suit the negotiating situation.

Before meeting with the people they're negotiating with, expert negotiators gather information about the people involved and about the negotiating situation. They know information is power. As they collect information and get ready to meet with the others, they think through the bargaining process. They think about what they want, how they will ask for it, and how they will react to other people's positions and requests. Then, they think through the reactions their requests or offers will elicit. They think through the consequences of their words and actions. And they plan how they want negotiations to proceed. I find the most effective way to begin preparing for a negotiation is to concentrate on two key areas: Know your own position and know your negotiating counterparts' positions.

## • Where Do I Stand?

Knowing your own position is more than saying to your self, "I want a 30 percent raise, and I want it now!" Most positions have many more components than the apparent issue that is driving people to the bargaining table. Before getting into the crossfire of negotiation, take an inventory of your position.

### • Inventory Item 1: Know What You Want

Most people go into negotiations with only a vague idea of what they want. When I say, "know what you want, " I mean know *exactly* what you want. Have a detailed picture in your mind of what you want. Say you've been looking for a job, and one company you're interested in has called you back to four interviews. You've been invited back once more, and this time you're confident they'll offer you a position. Some people think to themselves: "I'll be anxious to see what they offer me. I hope the salary and benefits are good. It'd be nice if I could get two weeks of vacation. I wonder exactly what position they'll want to give me." That's not the way to do it if you plan to get what you want.

When you go back for that final interview, you need to know more than simply that you want the job. Have a clear picture of what you want from the company. You might have a list that goes something like this:

- I want the position of director of creative design.
- I want $75,000 a year.
- I want creative license to pursue projects without interference from superiors at every turn.
- I expect two weeks of vacation, all major holidays, and five personal leave days.
- I want full insurance benefits.

Your demands must be specific to carry any negotiating power. Specific demands give you strength. You have a clear goal to shoot for. You're more confident when you present your proposal. And the force with which you state your position can have a positive effect on how others will respond to it.

Sometimes simply acting like you expect the answer to be yes, or that the other party or person will agree with you, can sway a person's decision in your favor. Although you can't rely solely on the force of your requests to get what you want in life, every little bit helps.

So, know exactly what you want when you're negotiating any important issues.

### • Inventory Item 2: Know When to Compromise
What if you don't get exactly what you ask for? Do you snap your briefcase shut and go home? No way! It's rare to get exactly what

you ask for. In fact, if you get everything you ask for, you're probably not asking for enough. Remember that negotiation is a give-and-take process, so be prepared to give up a little. But to avoid giving up too much or giving in on the wrong issues, know in advance what concessions and compromises you are willing to make.

If your attitude is "Let's put our heads together and see if we can work out something," you'll probably give up more than if you had set certain limits on how far and in what areas you would compromise.

To be an effective negotiator, you have to do more than expect to make concessions in general. You need to know going in what you want to walk away with. You need to plan exactly what concessions you're willing to make.

Whenever I'm negotiating, I go in with three levels of objectives:

1. I know what I must have,
2. I know what I would like to have, and
3. I know what it would be great to have.

I start off the negotiations trying to get what it would be great to have. But we don't always get our wishes in this life, so I'm prepared to start whittling away at my desires, if I have to. And to be sure I don't whittle too closely, I run through every conceivable "what if"scenario.

Let's go back to the job offer example. OK, you decided you want the job as director of creative design. In your mind, you've outlined your desires: creative freedom, a salary of $75,000 a year, a full insurance package, two weeks' vacation, paid holidays, and ample personal leave. That would be great to have.

You walk confidently in to your interview. The company president tells you that you're the candidate of choice and they'd like to bring you on board. After exchanging a few pleasantries about feeling positive toward the company, you unveil your list of desires. Almost immediately the prospective employer fires off a counteroffer.

The company wants to hire you as a creative designer rather than as director. Instead of heading a small staff you would work independently of others. And instead of $75,000, they present a figure of $65,000.

What do you do?

Now is not the time to begin figuring in your head if you can afford to accept a $65,000 offer. All that needs to be thought out ahead of time. If you've done enough "what if" scenarios, you already know that offering you $10,000 less a year is a possibility, and you're not caught off guard when it happens.

If you've thought it through, you might be able to come back with a counteroffer of your own. For instance, you might say, "No, I couldn't accept $65,000, but I could live with $70,000." Or it might be that the perks and benefits package is good enough that you could settle for $68,000.

Anticipating compromises and planning exactly how far you are willing to cut back on your demands helps you maintain a strong negotiating position. By planning ahead of time, you keep your confidence from getting shaken when you start making adjustments. You know how far you can reduce your demands, so there's no reason to get uptight. You won't panic.

Secondly, having a realistic bottom line prevents you from accepting an offer that you might live to regret. After doing some investigating on the cost of living in that area, you might have learned that you can't afford to work for that company for less than $72,000 a year. You can use your research to back up any claims you make. You can say, "I calculated what the commute to your office would cost me. If you look at these figures, I think you'll have to agree that I would be losing money by accepting $65,000 a year." Calculate your limits before entering negotiations, and you won't get burned when you start making concessions.

### • Inventory Item 3: Always Have Alternatives

Have alternatives to your ultimate goal, just in case you can't negotiate an acceptable agreement. What if the prospective employer doesn't agree to minimum terms? What if that $72,000 figure is just too high for the company? Do you come down or do you walk away?

Always be prepared to walk away. Let me remind you of a gold nugget of negotiating: Never want anything too badly. Desperation will cause you to make a bad deal every time. That's why I always try to have alternatives to my ultimate goal. For every plan A, always have a plan B. Knowing your bottom line protects you from making bad decisions; so does having an alternative.

Your alternative to accepting the creative design job could be to stay in your present job and keep looking. If you're out of work, can you get by on temporary work or freelancing until a better job offer comes along? Or can you accept the job on a trial basis, with the option of earning a raise in three months? If you take the time to plan, you will usually find you have several options. Situations are seldom as desperate as they seem. Just think about them before you meet with prospective employers.

Having an alternative is like having a safety net in case negotiations don't go the way you've planned them. That's the secret of being able to think fast. Don't feel obligated to accept an agreement solely on the other party's terms. I've been offered jobs that I simply couldn't afford to accept. If the prospective employers couldn't meet my bottom-line figure, I thanked them for their time and went on my way. For a couple of days I would find myself hoping they would call and tell me they had reconsidered and that, of course, I was worth every penny I was asking for. That never happened. I survived.

The only way you can negotiate like a pro is to know, in advance, exactly what you'll do if things don't work out like you want. And always be prepared to walk away. It takes guts, but it makes you a powerful negotiator.

Remember, the person who cares the least about the outcome always has the strongest negotiating position. The less willing you are to walk away, the more vulnerable you are. Think about it—aside from the casualties of unproductive peace talks, most negotiations aren't fatal—even when they fall through. Most top-notch negotiators know that every negotiation involves a calculated risk, so they always calculate their risks in advance.

Knowing in advance what you want and where you're willing to compromise strengthens your negotiating position. You have confidence in your position, and you know that you have other options. You will be much less likely to accept a bad deal. But thorough preparation for negotiation involves more than taking an inventory of your own position. You also need to know what's going on in the camp of the people with whom you're negotiating. You need to survey your negotiation opponents' positions, uncovering their strengths and weaknesses as much as possible.

## • What Is My Counterpart's Position?

Before sitting down to negotiate, I always try to find the answers to the questions described in the following section.

### • Question 1: What Do They Want?

You know what you want, but what do the people you're negotiating with want? They are coming to the table with their own agenda. Let's say you're representing an employee who has filed a grievance accusing management of singling her out for the more difficult jobs in her division. She believes she's being harassed and she wants it to stop. But what does management want? Ask them what their position is. You may discover that the woman's charges shocked her supervisor. He thought the woman wanted more responsibility. He had been giving her the jobs because she was his most dependable employee. What he wants is at least one person in the department he can rely on to accept some responsibility and keep things running smoothly.

Discovering what the other side wants is crucial to arriving at satisfactory agreements. Once you discover that management wants to groom the employee for more responsibility, you can focus on working out terms for possible pay increase or promotion, instead of simply demanding that management treat all its employees equally. So, always try to determine what the other side wants.

### • Question 2: What Is Important to the Other Side?

A couple may want the house you're selling, but what's really important to them? Is it the location? Is it the fact that they can assume your loan? If you know what features or terms are important to them, you can use those points to negotiate for the features or terms that are important to you.

### • Question 3: Why Are They Willing to Negotiate, and Why Now?

During the Paris peace talks between the United States and North Vietnam in 1968, the Vietnamese delegation brought with them one extremely valuable piece of information about the U.S. government. They knew why the United States was anxious to negotiate. Lyndon Johnson's administration was under tremendous pressure to reach an agreement by the fall, when a general election was scheduled. The Democrats needed a peace treaty if they wanted to stay in the White House.

So, what did the Vietnamese do? They killed time with stunts like haggling over the size and shape of the bargaining table. In essence, they pushed the United States to the wall until our country's negotiator was forced to give up almost everything in an attempt to end the fighting in Vietnam (from Roger Dawson's *You Can Get Anything You Want*, Regency Books, Inc., pages 107–108).

### • Question 4: What Does the Other Side Bring to the Negotiating Situation?

Before you get into negotiations with people, find out what they have to offer you. Do they have anything you want? I don't see much point in negotiating with someone who only wants something from you, unless that person has something you want.

## • *Question 5: What Resources Does Your Opponent Have?*

In other words, do the people you're negotiating with have other options? A customer, for example, usually has other options when negotiating with a salesperson. The customer can usually shop elsewhere. But in some negotiations, you may be the only source for the item the people you're negotiating with want. Either way, determine what options your counterparts have. How badly do they need this deal? Are they desperate? I don't have to tell you that the more desperate they are and the more badly they need the deal, the better the chances are that you will get what you want.

The more you know about the people you're negotiating with and the better you understand their needs, the more control you will have at the bargaining table.

## • Information Is Power

Remember, information is power. It's amazing what you can find out just by doing a little investigative work. If you're trading for a new car, for instance, you can buy a magazine that will tell you exactly how much markup the dealer has on the car and how much profit he has on every option installed. Your banker can tell you how much your old car is worth. Asking a few questions can save you thousands of dollars.

And, speaking of cars, one of the classic examples of the power of knowledge comes from the automobile industry. Before Chrysler's Lee Iacocca went to the U.S. Congress to request the largest government loan guarantee ever given a private company, he was armed to the teeth with the right kinds of information. For example, Iacocca knew that many of the members of Congress were opposed to the idea of the government bailing out private enterprises. That was an ideological position he could not hope to affect solely by presenting logical arguments. He had to find a way to present his case in terms that would get the attention of every congressional representative.

What did he do? He instructed his accounting people to research the actual economic impact of a Chrysler bankruptcy on each congressional district in the entire country. He learned that out of the 535 districts, only two had no Chrysler dealers or suppliers.

Iacocca then presented a detailed computer printout to each representative demonstrating the financial impact a Chrysler bankruptcy would have in his or her district. He showed them the number of people who would be thrown out of work, what the net loss in annual payroll would be, and the cost in local and state taxes. He painted a clear picture for the representatives of exactly what their constituents would lose if the loan guarantee did not come through. He also made that information available to the local news media in each of the affected districts.

Needless to say, he got the representative's attention, and he got his $1.5 billion loan. Many political experts say that, more than any other single factor, giving the members of Congress the bottom line on their districts is what turned the tide in favor of Chrysler's plea for a loan guarantee.

I could tell you hundreds of stories to show how good negotiators have gotten what they wanted simply by going in with the right information. So, collect enough of the right kinds of information, and you can greatly influence the outcome of the negotiations.

## • Position Yourself for Maximum Advantage

Your position is the way others perceive you and your negotiating strength. You can position yourself as a strong, ethical negotiator, or you can position yourself as a weak victim. It's all up to you. You control the mental perceptions others hold of you and what you represent. There is often a big difference in the way you perceive yourself and the way you are perceived by others. Never assume that others see you as you see yourself. People always see you in relation to the way they see themselves and the world. And people always evaluate the value of what you have to offer in relation to all the other people they could negotiate with.

At least 75 percent of the way you are perceived comes from nonverbal communication—the way you look, the way you act, your gestures and facial expressions, and your tone of voice. Often, people are less concerned about what you say and do than they are about the way you say and do it.

So, you can affect (either positively or negatively) the way you are positioned in the minds of those you negotiate with. Choose your words carefully. Focus on clarity and precision in your speech. State your position firmly, carry yourself with confidence, and position yourself as a person with negotiating power.

## One Last Thought . . .

### Six Steps for Negotiation Preparation

The most commonly overlooked aspect of negotiation is preparation. We say things like, "We're just in the negotiation stage of the deal . . . ." There is no more profitable expenditure of time than the time spent preparing to negotiate. Here's your checklist:

1. *Know what you want and don't want.* Most of us have a general idea of what we want or want to avoid in a deal. Unfortunately, general objectives tend to render general results, leading to second guessing and dissatisfaction. Instead, write a paragraph describing in detail what you want and don't want from the transaction, then, edit this description furiously until it is laser focused and precise. When we are crystal clear on our objective(s) and rationale(s) for their acquisition, we are most likely to achieve desired results.

2. *Know what your counterpart wants and doesn't want.* Now do the same for your counterpart. Write the description of what your opposite is looking for and seeking to avoid. This exercise tends to be a real stumper and eventually a real eye-opener. Knowing our counterpart's goals, objectives, and sought after results helps us see commonalities that lead to creative solutions.

3. *Know what concessions you are willing to give.* What must you absolutely achieve to consummate a successful bargain? What terms, conditions, and extras could you live without? Every great negotiator knows there must be give and take on both sides for agreements that make sense.

4. *Know your alternatives.* Remember when you bought your first car? Mine was a 1956 T-Bird. The guy I bought mine from told me, "I like you and want to sell you the car, but there's another person coming over in 30 minutes who also wants the car." Wow, did the dynamics of the negotiation shift on the spot. Having an alternative vendor or supplier really helps your level of confidence.

5. *Know your counterpart and your subject matter.* A lot of information is available to us on personality styles, body language, and neurolinguistic programming. Remember, transactions take place between people and people view the same facts and appeals differently. Subject matter is simple. Know it cold— there is no excuse for being ill informed. Lost credibility is rarely recovered.

6. *Rehearse.* You know how to get to Carnegie Hall! It's the same road to negotiation success—practice, practice, practice. Attend swap meets and flea markets. They are wonderful opportunities to sharpen your skills. Remember—use it or lose it!

Most negotiators rarely, if ever, thoroughly prepare to negotiate. But this is the magic! Try this checklist before you negotiate. Your returns will improve dramatically.

· · · ·

# Negotiate on the Same Wavelength

WITHOUT COMMUNICATION—AND I MEAN MIND-TO-MIND, HEART-to-heart communication-negotiation doesn't happen. As a matter of fact, poor communication is almost always the cause of failed negotiations between people who sincerely want to settle on a solution that's fair to everyone. As an attorney, I've seen volatile and hotly disputed cases drag on for months, even years, because the people involved couldn't communicate. A large percentage of the civil and small-claims cases clogging our legal system can be traced back to poor communication. The people involved just can't seem to get together.

Some negotiations fail because the people involved aren't committed to negotiating ethically or in good faith.

Cheating, lying, or blatant attempts to manipulate can bring almost any negotiation to a screeching halt. When honest, intelligent people are involved, however, if problems crop up, it's because of a breakdown in communications. To negotiate effectively, people have to be able relate to one another, to share a meeting of meanings to cut through the smoke screens that hinder understanding. People have to operate on the same wavelength if they hope to negotiate a productive agreement.

## • Understanding the Complexities of Interpersonal Communication

Communication isn't as simple a process as you might imagine. I think most people see communication as one person talking, then pausing to let someone else talk. It would be nice if making ourselves understood and understanding others were as simple as saying words and listening to voices. Communication, however, is much more complicated than that.

Communication involves people exchanging ideas, expressing emotions, and reaching new levels of understanding together. Messages must have meaning and people must convey those meanings to others. Communication is a complex endeavor, especially at the bargaining table, which is usually cluttered with emotion, tension, and ambitions. You'll experience the barriers to communication listed in the following sections in your negotiations.

### • *Barrier 1: Emotions*

When people let their emotions rule their words and actions, they get so caught up in what they want that they sometimes fail to express themselves clearly and they stop listening to what others have to say. I call that monologue in duet. That's where two people keep talking in turns without acknowledging each other's comments. Talking without listening to what others are saying is one of the biggest barriers to communication in negotiations.

Husbands and wives fall into this trap all the time. They may hear the words the other is saying, but they completely ignore the meanings behind the words. For example, a couple is considering buying a new car. The woman wants a pickup truck; the man wants a sporty little coupe. So, the wife starts working on her husband. She says, "We don't need another car. You have a company car, and my car is only two years old. We haven't even finished paying for it. Buying a car right now is a waste of money."

The whole time she's ranting about how useless another car would be, her husband is agreeing with her. He's saying things like, "You're right . . . what do we need with another car? It would just be another monthly payment. And the insurance rates on new cars are out of this world."

If she were listening to his responses, she would realize that her argument is too good. She doesn't really hear what he is saying. As a matter of fact, her arguments are so convincing, he concludes they don't need a new vehicle at all. She is so intent on having her say that she doesn't notice when he switches from debating about whether to buy a truck or a car to questioning whether they should buy a new vehicle of any kind. She is so driven by her position that she talks her husband out of what he wants and out of what she wants. How effectively would you say she communicated? She did a great job of getting the wrong point across, which is a little like the classic medical report that said, "The operation was a success, but the patient died." She focused on making her husband understand what she didn't want, rather than expressing clearly what she did want. This is a common mistake. If she had listened to her husband's input throughout their discussion, she would have caught herself before it was too late. The way it ended up, neither of them will get what they want—a new vehicle.

Commonly, the individuals negotiating are too emotionally involved in winning. They have a difficult time looking at the negotiations objectively as a means to benefit both sides. They focus on getting their way, rather than on expressing their needs and interests in a way that leads to solutions. And their self-focusing prevents them from listening to what anyone else has to say. Thus, they don't communicate and they don't make progress in negotiations.

To communicate—and negotiate—effectively, we have to learn to let go of our emotions and concentrate on making ourselves understood and on understanding others.

### • *Barrier 2: Misperceptions*

When I look out my window, I may see a partly cloudy sky, while you see a partly sunny day. All of us perceive the world and its contents differently. Our individual experiences, our feelings, our values, and our needs color the words and phrases we hear and use with different shades of meaning. For example, the word "expensive" might not mean the same thing to you that it does to me. I know it doesn't mean the same thing to my wife that it does to me.

Differing perceptions can wreak havoc on the communication process. For example, some sources report that after the explosion of the space shuttle *Challenger* in 1986, investigators discovered that several engineers had tried to warn management that the mission was in jeopardy. But the engineers' laid-back style had made their messages seem anything but urgent. Management had felt that if the engineers were really worried, they would have been more emphatic about their concerns. So no one listened. Seven people died, and the American space program suffered a setback it's still struggling to overcome.

Management misread the engineers' conservative style. You know how type-A management people panic when something's about to go wrong. They think everybody else is the same way. So when the engineers seemed to be calm as they expressed their doubts, the managers didn't think the problem was serious. They perceived their laid-back style as a "no-need-to-worry" signal.

It's easy to see why misperceptions can cause serious problems in negotiations. When two people aren't talking about the same thing—which is basically what happens with mispercep-tions—they might as well be talking in different languages. How in the world can they agree on anything when they aren't even talking about the same thing?

To negotiate effectively, we have to be able to align the differ-ing perceptions of the individuals involved in negotiations. And concentrating intently on sending and receiving messages accu-rately is the only way we can overcome the misperceptions that block most communication attempts.

## • *Barrier 3: Smoke Screens*

A smoke screen is anything that clouds the real issues at stake in a negotiation. Smoke screens block communication because they obscure what's really going on inside a person's head or heart. Sometimes, people throw up smoke screens unintentionally. They don't realize they are muddying the water with nonissues. They don't have a clear grasp of the situation and they might offer proposals that seem to sidestep the main focus of the nego-tiations.

For example, let's say you are debating with a worker about who will present a report on the latest research development to the vice president of marketing. Your colleague says to you, "Well, if I give the report this time, you can give it next time." That person might think that seems fair. But who says there's going to be a next time? Maybe you won't have another opportu-nity to work together. Talking about the "next time" is a nonissue and it only complicates matters. Stick with the present situation and design a solution with the information and resources you have now.

Other times, people will spew out a smoke screen to distract or mislead you. Remember, knowledge is power. Some people think that if they withhold information or misinform you, they will have an advantage over you. I have two excellent tactics for clearing away smoke screens. The first is to ask, "Why do you say that?" when you sense someone is trying to cloud the issues. For example, the person you're negotiating with might say, "I don't believe the price you've set is fair." By questioning your integrity, the person might be trying to force you to lower your price. Don't fall for it. Simply ask, "Why do you say that?" and pull the discussion back to the real issues.

Another effective tactic for clearing up the confusion that comes from a smoke screen is to state your understanding of a person's meaning, then ask, "Is that what you are saying?" You can say, for example, "You think the price is too high. Is that what you are saying?" From that point, you can pull the discussion back to the value versus the cost. If the buyer really believes your price is too high, have that person explain to you what makes him think so. Has he seen similar items for less? Is he not convinced of its value? Or could it be that he just doesn't have the money? Asking someone to explain his statements forces him to describe exactly what's going on inside his mind. Watch out for smoke screens that get in the way of effective communication.

## • How to Get Results through Improved Communication

Considering the obstacles we face, it's not surprising that most of us don't communicate as effectively as we could. We are not doomed, however, to muddled messages and mixed meanings. With a conscious effort, we can overcome the barriers that block understanding in negotiation. We can become better at getting our messages across and working together toward a common goal—a satisfactory agreement.

I have several rules that I follow to help me connect with others at the negotiating table and in all forms of communication.

### • Rule 1: Organize Your Thoughts

You need to have a general idea of what you're going to say when you start negotiating. Try outlining the main points you want to cover. Writing down my thoughts in advance helps me express them more clearly once the pressure of negotiating cranks up.

Have you ever sat in on a trial? There are some big differences between the real thing and the Hollywood dramatics that unfold on television programs and in the movies. For instance, television lawyers sit with their hands folded on a table free of papers and clutter. When questioning witnesses or giving their summations, they pace back and forth in front of the jury. Reality follows a different script.

Most lawyers have tons of notes in front of them and bulging out of their briefcases. When it comes time for opening or closing remarks, a lot of attorneys practically read straight from their notes. I'm not kidding. Only the more experienced, more daring lawyers stray far from the table where they have their crib sheets laid out. They realize there is too much at stake to be careless. They know that every word counts, and they want to make themselves clear.

Planning the gist of what you will say is the most effective way to avoid sending mixed or muddled messages. Don't just outline your plans before you get started, but keep doing it as you go along. Any time you're going to speak, stop and think about what you're going to say and how you're going to say it. When someone says something to you that demands a response, think before you reply.

There's no law that says every statement must be met with a response within five seconds. As a matter of fact, a little silence can be your strongest negotiating tool. Just make sure that what you're about to say will clearly and concisely express what you mean. Stop whenever you feel the need and reorganize your thoughts before you respond to anything that happens or is said. I've seen people use this technique very effectively. They'll say something like, "Of course, you understand that I'm going to have to research this and get back to you on it." Once they've bought a little time, they can think through what they're going to say in response. That tactic not only helps you organize what you're going to say, it helps you digest the meaning of what someone else has proposed.

## • Rule 2: Think Through What You Will Say; Don't Just Think About It

The difference between thinking something through and thinking about it is a crucial distinction in communication. Thinking about something leads to confusion; thinking it through leads to clarity.

In the early 1990s, a colleague of mine spent a great deal of time in Russia trying to help businesses set up trade links to take advantage of the new openness of Perestroika and Glasnost. He told me there is an enormous difference between the way most Americans negotiate and the Russian style of negotiation. One of the quirks of Russian negotiators is that they always ask themselves, "If we do or say this, what will it cause the other party to do or say in response?" Because they think this way, they can usually predict almost exactly what the Western response will be to anything they do or say at the negotiating table.

We Americans tend to take the opposite approach. For us, it's enough for us to "tell it like it is" and "let the chips fall where they may." Maybe it's because of the strong value we place on telling the truth. But there's obviously wisdom in the Russian approach. You process an idea through to its logical conclusion by evaluating the possible responses you may get from the other side.

Don't be put off by the amount of speculation you'll have to do. All of us constantly make certain assumptions, based on reasonably good information. If we didn't, we'd never get anywhere in life.

For example, if I make an offer and say, "Take it or leave it," what kind of response is that most likely to produce? The other party could say, "Okay, we'll take it." They could say, "Thanks, but no thanks." They could say, "We won't take it, but here's what we would accept." Or they could say, "Nobody talks to us that way!" and pull out a gun and start shooting. That's a range of possibilities you can process through. If, based on your experience with the other party, you believe there's a good chance they would either accept your offer or come up with a counteroffer, it makes sense to say, "Take it or leave it." If you're negotiating with a crazy gunman who's holding a hostage, it might not be the best thing to say.

Give some thought to what response you're most likely to get from what you are about to say, ask yourself if that's the most productive way to say it, and think through what you're going to do if you get certain types of responses. I know that sounds like a pretty complicated process, but we are talking about the way pros negotiate. How far you want to get into this is up to you. But believe me, the more carefully you think through what you are going to do and say, the more powerful you can become as a negotiator.

## • Rule 3: Always Recognize that Actions Speak Louder than Words

Experts say that at least 75 percent of communication is nonverbal. It has more to do with the way we look, what we do, and the way we say things than it does with what we actually say. For example, if I give you a big smile and say, "Hey, man, you'd better take it while I'm in a generous mood," that's one thing. But if I stand up, throw my offer on the table, say "There it is, take it or leave it!" and start walking toward the door, that sends a completely different message.

The best negotiators practice saying and doing things in ways that send precisely the messages they want to send. The bottom line is, the better you become at using nonverbal messages and reading the nonverbal messages others send, the more effective you can become as a communicator and a negotiator.

It's important not only to think through what you're going to say, but to think through the way you're going to say it. Everything you do is a part of the communication and negotiation process. Make sure that you don't send the wrong messages by doing something that conflicts with what you are saying. If, for instance, you've just told a salesperson you're not interested in what they're selling, don't sit there and read through the brochure you've just been handed. If you really mean you're not interested, stand up, hand the brochure back, and start leading the person toward the door.

### • Rule 4: Be Concise

Always get right to the point. Say what you mean in as few words as possible, without being blunt. If you drone on and on, people will stop listening to you. Then how can you get your message across? Always look for the most concise way to communicate your meaning clearly.

Give people the details, but just give them the meat of what you have to say upfront. Elaborate as they ask questions. You know you're not communicating very well when people start saying things like, "What's your point?" or "So what are you saying?" I've seen that happen and it's not a pretty sight.

According to *The Wall Street Journal*, the typical American receives an average of 5,000 invitations to buy every day. We all are bombarded with requests of all kinds, and with information we don't need or want. What do we do? We learn how to simply tune out the things we don't want to hear.

Since most people tune out a great deal of what we say, there are two techniques that can help us get our messages through the walls of defense. First, we have to oversimplify, and second, we have to repeat our messages until they sink in. For example, look at what Verizon does. In their commercials, the actor for Verizon walks around and says "Can you hear me now?" over and over into his cell phone. Now, that's a gross oversimplification. It's so oversimplified it's not technically accurate. But you get point and that's what matters. Then, Verizon takes that oversimplified message and repeats it time after time. Eventually, people do hear them and get the message.

If you want to boost your negotiating power, practice saying everything clearly and concisely, then repeat your key points again and again. One problem most of us encounter in negotiating is that other people get so caught up in their own concerns they don't pay attention to what we have to say. That's why it's vital to organize what we hope to say to make sure we get our main points across, and that we say them in the concise and compelling way.

### • Rule 5: Always Translate What You Have to Say into Benefits for the Listener

People will listen more carefully to what you're saying if they believe there is something in it for them. Focus on that something, even when you are stating what you want. For example, when you go for a job interview, don't talk about the big salary the company can pay you. Instead, talk about how much you'd be worth to the company. You try to convince them that they'll be ahead by hiring you, regardless of the cost. Or if you're selling something, you talk about the value of the item, not the cost. Always talk in terms of how the other parties are going to benefit from the negotiations.

### • Rule 6: Listen Intently to the Other Parties

Communicating effectively isn't talking until you beat another person into submission. It's stating exactly what you want in clear and concise terms, and then listening for a response. As basic as this sounds, it's amazing how few of us actually communicate that way. Most people would probably agree that the biggest problems we create for ourselves at the bargaining table result from talking too much and not listening enough. We've all done it at one time or another. We just get so caught up in our desire to make things go our way, we start talking and we don't know when to quit. That's no way to win at the negotiation table.

If you want to reach an agreement with others, you have to make sure that your desires are heard and understood. And that takes total concentration. You have to make sure you say what you really mean in a way that presents your case as strongly as possible. The other side of the coin is that it takes concentration to listen to others and to understand what they really mean.

Here are a few pointers for listening more effectively:

- *Open your mind.* Be receptive to what is being said. Don't judge the person speaking and don't critique his or her delivery or content. Focus on understanding the message.

- *Make a commitment to listen.* Begin listening as soon as the other person starts talking, not just when you happen to catch an interesting word or phrase.
- *Listen for facts and feelings.* There's usually more to messages than what meets the ear. Listen between the lines. How is the person feeling about what he or she is saying to you? What facts concern him or her most?
- *Eliminate or resist distractions.* Turn off any noise that might distract you, like a radio, television, or appliances. If you must contend with conversations the hall, close the door to the office. Don't let your mind wander to other activities or concerns in your life. When listening to another person, tune in to that person. Lock the rest of the world out of your mind.
- *Respond with questions for clarification.* Planning to ask questions forces you to pay attention to what others are saying.
- *Remember important points the speaker is making.* If appropriate, take notes.

As you increase your listening effectiveness, you increase your negotiating effectiveness. One reason is that you will collect more information that you can use in your search for solutions.

## • Two-Way Communication: The Key to Negotiating Effectively

Effective communication is a two-way street. People exchange messages, convey ideas and emotions, and seek to understand one another. If we want to negotiate like the pros, we need to be able to relate to one another on this level. Speak to be understood, and listen to understand. Organize your thoughts and tune in to the people with whom you're talking. Together you proceed to a new reality—and to a creative solution.

## One Last Thought . . .

# Gender Sense in Negotiation

Men and women have been talking to each other, past each other, and at each other ever since Adam and his rib parted ways to open the first gender gap. Our early ancestors settled on a division of labor, dictated largely by biological necessity: The women bore the children and carried their infants' first food supply within their bosoms. Hence, Mama stayed home with the kids while Papa went hunting Mastodons and fighting bad guys from other tribes. Mama dug up roots and picked berries to go with the meaty victuals Papa brought home, but outside she was an observer—not a participant—in the hunt.

From early history, boys and girls grew up in separate cultures, schooled in separate roles. Not surprisingly, men and women developed identifiable styles of communication. Papa's language was the language of the hunt and the fight—of competition. Mama's language was the language of hearth and home—of nurturing and cooperation. It should not surprise us that men and women frequently misunderstand one another, even in everyday communications.

As we approached modern times, girls were expected to learn the arts of housekeeping—cooking, sewing, and child-rearing—while boys were expected to learn trades or enter the professions. Men were expected to be strong and assertive while women were encouraged to be beautiful and submissive. Some women did embark on careers, but only those reserved for the "fairer sex," such as teaching, nursing, and occasionally, writing. But whatever role they chose, they were expected to be women first—virtuous, yielding, dainty, and pretty.

Throughout history, the strongest have made the rules, and until modern times the strong were the people with the muscles and agility—

the men. Women could negotiate, but only from positions of weakness, because men made the laws and had the brawn to enforce them.

Today strength still prevails, but power is no longer measured by the size of your biceps. Technology has leveled the playing field so that women can fly airplanes, drive 18-wheelers, and operate construction cranes as skillfully as men. They can also program computers, chart market trends, and plot corporate strategies with all the finesse that men can muster. They are joining the men in the hunt, and when the men try to force them away, they don't have to defend their status with a club, but rather the law. Increasingly, women are taking their places at corporate tables as fully participating executives. They are interacting with men as equals, not as subordinates. The "man's world" that used to exist has been evaporating—sometimes slowly, to be sure—ever since women won the right to vote.

Women have more than doubled their representation in noncleri-cal, white-collar jobs in American companies since the 1960s, and now occupy almost half these positions. However, a 1994 survey by *The Wall Street Journal* showed that women still held less than one-third of the managerial jobs in the 38,059 companies that reported to the U.S. Equal Employment Opportunity Commission in 1992, the latest year for which data were available. Among 200 of the nation's biggest companies analyzed by the *Journal*, women held just one-fourth of the jobs classified by the Equal Employment Opportunity Commission (EEOC) as "officials and managers"—a broad category that includes a wide variety of supervisory posts, from the manager of the janitorial service to the CEO of the company.

At the vice presidential level, women made up an even smaller percentage—less than 5 percent in 1990, according to Catalyst, a non-profit research group in New York that studies women in business.

Many women get the feeling that this preponderance of males in top positions creates a management culture that is hostile to females. Companies that do succeed in populating their executive suites with a sizable female contingent find that it becomes easier to attract able women.

The Sara Lee Corporation began hiring women into high-level jobs during the 1980s and, as *The Wall Street Journal* put it, "watched the cultural changes trickle down." The newspaper quoted Gary Grom, senior vice president of human resources: "The more women in top management jobs, the more women are attracted to them." The reason this is true is that women find it easier to relate to other women and men find it easier to relate to other men. Women often don't fit into the corporate culture, which was developed by and for men.

Wells Fargo has succeeded in changing its corporate culture into a blend of genders. By the early 1990s, about two-thirds of its management people were women. By 1992, seven of the 38 executive vice presidents and 19 of the 108 senior vice presidents were women.

Companies such as Sara Lee and Wells Fargo demonstrate that when a certain critical mass is achieved, the genders can form a successful blend.

The ideal situation—the one toward which we hope we are moving—would be a work force populated equally by men and women at all levels, with equal opportunity for all. In such an environment, men and women would develop a common language based on common activities. A language in which the best features of both are blended. This gender-blended language will enable men and women to communicate precisely and comfortably with one another, across the conference table, and across the dinner table. Gender-blending is already a work in progress.

• • • •

# Questions: The Most Powerful Tool of an Expert Negotiator

OPENING THE TWO-WAY STREET OF COMMUNICATION IN BARGAIN-ing is undoubtedly crucial to negotiating effectively. People must understand one another if they are to work together to design mutually satisfying agreements. Yet, getting people to open up and exchange information and feelings is also one of the most challenging aspects of negotiating like the pros.

An intangible, yet undeniably real, barrier separates people who sit down to negotiate. The bricks in this barrier are each individual's needs, desires, and goals for the event; the mortar between the bricks is fear of being taken advantage of. As I've said throughout this book, many people see negotiation as a winner-takes-all battle. So they come to the bargaining table with their defenses up. However, as long as this wall stands between people negotiating, they can't communicate on a level that will allow them to arrive at the best solution for everyone involved.

Fortunately, this wall is not impervious. We can tear it down, by using one of the most powerful tools of negotiation, questions. Skillfully asked questions can transform negotiations from an adversarial conflict to a partnership. By asking the right questions in the right way at the right time, you tap into people's inner feelings and you stimulate dialogue and, therefore, understanding. By asking the right questions, you can lead the people involved in the negotiations to productive agreements.

Using questions to facilitate the negotiating process, however, involves more than firing off an armload of inquiries and pumping people for information. To create understanding and build relationships, you must understand the dynamics of asking questions, and you must develop appropriate interview skills.

## • Controlling the Information Balance

Usually, when people are preparing to negotiate they spend the majority of their time thinking about what they're going to say and how they're going to say it. It's crucial that you have a solid outline of what you plan to say. You want to make sure you're going to cover all your points. I've found, however, that an ineffective negotiator gives little thought to uncovering the other parties' motives, fears, and desires. Don't get caught in that trap.

I've spent years negotiating and studying the negotiating process. I can tell you that one trait most poor negotiators share is that they talk entirely too much. They tell everything they know, and end up giving the other parties all kinds of information, which the other side can use against them.

Expert negotiator Gary Karrass offers a perfect example involving an aerospace firm, the federal government, and a multi-million-dollar contract. Because of the complexity and tremendous importance of the deal, the aerospace firm sent a team of engineers and salespeople to negotiate the transaction.

The salespeople were using every technique in the book to keep the price up. They focused on the point that their bid was justified because a portion of the project would be difficult to complete. They pulled out charts and graphs, and pointed to facts and figures. They emphasized the cost of specialized production.

Suddenly, one of the engineers, who was there simply to answer technical questions, commented, "Well, it won't be that difficult" (from Gary Karrass, *Negotiate to Close*, Simon & Schuster, 1987, page 76).

You can be sure the salespeople were probably ready to kill him. I'll bet the people in that room could actually hear the price drop. This proves my point: the more you talk, the more likely you are to sabotage your own efforts. So be careful about how much information you give the other side. Certainly, it's important to state your proposal clearly and to help the other side understand your position. But be careful not to reveal information that weakens your position.

I would even suggest that you make a list of classified information before you get into negotiations. Think about any information that could be dangerous if it were to fall into the wrong hands. For example, if a negotiating counterpart knows you're operating on a tight deadline, he or she has a strong weapon to use against you. Make a note to yourself not to mention deadlines or time pressures. Know what information you don't want your negotiating opponents to have, or at least the information you don't want to hand to them on a silver platter. That way, you'll be less likely to accidentally spill your guts when you're face-to-face with them.

If you want to negotiate from a position of power at the bargaining table, learn to control the balance of information by asking questions effectively. You can uncover vital information without giving away clues about your weaknesses or strengths. By asking questions, you make sure your opponent will talk more, and you'll talk less. And that's only one of the great bene-fits of asking questions during negotiations. There are several, including the following.

- The right kinds of questions asked in the right way at exactly the right time can often give you complete control of the negotiating process.
- You will gather more information from others and reveal less about yourself. Information is power, and the most effective way to collect information is to ask questions.
- You can use questions to deflect heat, or to put the heat on your negotiating opponent.
- You can use questions to gather useful information, or to give information, if you do it cleverly enough.
- The right questions open up communication between you and the other parties. Open communication usually means increased trust, and trust is the foundation of a team working together for mutual benefits.

Learning to ask questions effectively could be one of the most profitable skills you'll ever acquire.

### • *The Perils of Probing*

Asking questions puts you in control of the negotiating process. Watch any of the prime-time news programs, like *60 Minutes* or *20/20*. When one of those master interviewers is talking with a subject, who do you think is in control? It's Mike Wallace or Barbara Walters, right? And all they're doing is asking questions and asking for clarification. What about in court? Who's in con-trol of the cross-examination during a trial? The witness who is answering questions, or the lawyer who's asking them?

As you were reading my questions, where did your answers take you? Through a series of questions, I led you to a planned conclusion: that questions put you in control.

Yes, questions can be extremely powerful. But, like any powerful tool, questions can also pose some hazards. The fol-lowing sections describe a few dangers to avoid when asking questions.

**Danger 1: Questions can threaten or offend the people with whom you're talking.** There is the danger that your timing or the way you ask your question will upset the people with whom you're negotiating. Let me share with you a classic story I heard about a barber who had been converted at a hellfire and brimstone church service one night. The next day, still excited about his experience, this barber figured he'd share his revelations with his customers. The first customer came in for a shave. Just as the barber placed the edge of a straight razor against the man's throat, he asked him, "Are you prepared to meet God?" (from Nido Qubein, *Professional Selling Techniques*, Farnsworth Publishing Co., 1983, page 126). Legend has it that the customer hasn't stopped running yet. It might have been a good question, but the barber's timing was terrible, and the way he asked it was even worse.

Seriously, though, you do have to be sensitive to the way people will react to your questions. The act of asking questions can be perceived as a threatening gesture in itself. When someone starts asking questions, our immediate response is, "Why do you want to know?" So, give careful consideration to the types of questions you ask, and phrase them in positive, nonthreatening terms.

**Danger 2: Questions can set people off on tangents.** I once asked a car salesperson how long he'd been selling cars for a living. I figured his answer would give me an idea of his negotiation skills. Would you believe that guy spent 20 minutes giving me a complete rundown of his career since he started mowing lawns in eighth grade? You can't always avoid this problem, but you can try to avoid asking questions that trigger most people to become talking machines. For instance, try not to ask questions about politics, religion, or sports, since most people can chat endlessly about such subjects. Keep your questions focused on the issues you are negotiating. If you discover you have a talker on your hands, be prepared to interrupt. Also, look out for people who try to beat you into submission by talking endlessly.

Don't give in just because you don't want to listen to the person ramble on any longer.

**Danger 3: Questions can trigger negative feelings.** For example, asking a buyer what he or she can afford can cause that person to focus on a purchase in terms of money going out, instead of on the benefits he or she will be gaining. The better question would be, "How much were you planning to invest?" Always try to phrase your questions in a way that builds positive feelings.

## • How to Ask Questions Effectively

Questions open up communication and encourage people to share information. That way, they can move from their individual positions and focus on ways to pool their strengths to form a mutually beneficial and satisfactory agreement.

Using questions, however, to uncover information and to break down barriers at the negotiating table is not as simple as getting into the bargaining situation and making up questions as you go along. Formulating effective questions requires forethought and skill.

The following sections provide a few guidelines for asking effective questions.

### • *Guideline 1: Plan Your Questions Ahead of Time*

It's crucial to formulate in advance the key questions you're going to ask. And you have to know how to ask questions once you get into a negotiating situation.

Try to figure out before you go in exactly what issues you'll be negotiating. Researching the people you're negotiating with, their organizations, and everything else relating to the negotiating situation enables you to formulate the right questions to get more information.

Think about the kind of answers you want. There's an old story about a trial lawyer who was cross-examining a witness to a fight. He asked the witness, "Were you there when the alleged

fight started?" The witness answered, "No." The lawyer continued, "Is it true that you didn't even arrive on the scene until after
the scuffle was over?"

"Yes, that's correct," the witness said.

Triumphantly, the defense attorney turned to the witness
abruptly and demanded, "Then how do you know my client bit
off part of the plaintiff's ear?"

The witness replied, "Because I saw him spit it out" (from
Gerard I. Nierenberg's *Fundamentals of Negotiating,* Harper-
Collins, 1987). That's what's known as a backfire, and I've seen
it happen in negotiations hundreds of times. The only way to
avoid it is to plan carefully. Think through the questions you will
ask and the possible responses they are likely to elicit.

You have to understand the types of people with whom
you'll be negotiating:

- What are they like?
- Are they experienced negotiators?
- Are they more likely to trust you or mistrust you? What's
  at stake for them in your negotiations?

The more you know the more effective your questions will be.

Plan in advance the questions that are likely to produce the
most information and have the greatest impact on moving you
and the people you negotiate with closer to a solution.

### • Guideline 2: Ask Permission to Ask Questions

Asking questions can sometimes put people on the defensive.
Avoid this by saying something like, "So that I can understand
where you're coming from and how we might work more closely
together, it would help me if I could ask you a few questions. Is
that OK with you?"

Make people feel like they are being interviewed, not interrogated. And once you have permission, ask your question gen-
tly. Instead of asking, "Why do you insist on those terms?" you
might say, "So I can better understand your position, can you
please explain to me why those terms are so important to you?"

The last thing you want to do is to put your opponents on the defensive. You want them to open up and let the information flow.

### • Guideline 3: Begin with Broad, Simple Questions and Progress to More In-Depth Questions

Start with open-ended questions. For example, "Tell me, what is your goal for these negotiations?" A question that broad doesn't pin anyone down. The other party will probably answer in general terms and not feel as if you're asking them to reveal their negotiating strategy. As you and the people you're negotiating with become more comfortable, move on to more narrow, direct questions. A good example of a direct question is, "How much do you want to be paid?" Direct questions give you specific information, facts, and figures.

As you uncover the facts surrounding the negotiations, you can gradually progress to positioning and strategic questions. A strategic question moves the parties in the direction of an agreement. An example might be, "What would it take for you to agree to our offer?" Questions like that help people focus on working out an acceptable arrangement. The person who asks these kinds of questions is also getting others to name their terms first, which can be extremely helpful in negotiations.

### • Guideline 4: Make Your Questions Easy

Ask questions that are easy to answer. In other words, don't ask questions that will make the people you're negotiating with feel uncomfortable. And don't ask questions that you think they don't know how to answer. Don't ask personal questions, unless they are absolutely vital to your negotiations. For example, "How much money do you make?" is a personal question. A real estate agent, however, has a valid reason for asking this question.

Also, if someone asks you a question you don't know the answer to, admit it. Learn how to say those magical little words "I don't know!" People seldom like to do this, but making up answers can get you into big trouble.

### • Guideline 5: Once You've Asked a Question, Be Quiet and Listen

This guideline may seem like an obvious tactic when you're asking questions, but that's not how most people communicate when they are negotiating. Party A asks a question. As party B proceeds to answer the question, party A is thinking about what he'll say next. I called that "monologue in duet" in a previous chapter. I've seen that little dance ruin more negotiating opportunities than I can count. I've also witnessed negotiations where someone answered his own question. A colleague of mine was plea bargaining with an assistant district attorney (DA). He wanted his client's charges reduced from driving while impaired to reckless driving. My friend asked, "Are you intent on making my client serve jail time?" Before the assistant DA had a chance to respond, the defense attorney said, "Certainly, people have served time for lesser offenses, but I think you have to look at the mitigating factors in my client's case."

I see two problems with the way my friend handled that situation. First, he answered his own question. Second, he handed his opponent a loaded gun. He didn't have to say anything about others being penalized for lesser offenses. This is a classic example of an open mouth causing serious problems.

If we want to get information from the people with whom we're negotiating, we have to listen. We have to concentrate on what they're saying, and to think about how what they're saying affects the negotiations.

### • Guideline 6: Use Questions to Give Information

The easiest way to give information with a question is to simply turn a statement into a question. For example, you might say, "Did you know that our company out-sold its closest competitor by 125 percent last year?" That can be an effective way to get information across without sounding pushy or overbearing. Also, framing a statement in the form of a question encourages people to respond with more information of their own.

For example, the other party might have responded to that statement with something like, "Yes, and we were quite impressed with your company's record of consistently outperforming its competitors. The last company we dealt with seemed to struggle to keep up. That caused us a lot of problems." That response tells you that they know how good you are, and that to them, your stability is an important issue.

## • *Guideline 7: Use Questions to Clarify*

I talked earlier about the necessity for clarification in the negotiating process. It's not uncommon for people to think they are agreeing to one thing only to find out later that they've agreed to something entirely different.

Use questions to clarify exactly what's expected of you and to make sure your negotiating partners understand what's expected of them. Experienced negotiators always ask enough questions to make sure that all parties agree on what is expected of them.

One important area of clarification is defining the terms you and your counterparts are using. Let's say you've just agreed to buy a new television set, and the salesperson tells you the total price is $595. What does that mean? Does it include taxes? Delivery charges? Set-up fees? To the dealer, the term "total price" may mean only the base cost of the product. But to you it might mean total, as in all the money it would take to have that one-eyed monster set up in your house. You could be talking about over a hundred dollars' worth of difference in definition of terms.

Obviously, that's a very simple example, but it's the principle I'm trying to get across. If somebody says they'll deliver your purchase on the first, what do they mean? The first of the month? Which month? On the first payment you make? On the first chance they get? This may sound nit-picky to you, but I've seen people lose a hundred grand or more by not defining terms carefully enough. I've known lawyers who would argue for days in court and cite dozens of precedents trying to prove their interpretations of what terms actually mean.

Keep asking questions until you are sure that you and those you're negotiating with mean precisely the same things by the terms you use. Let me share a warning with you: Be extremely careful about clarifying terms if all the parties seem to agree on a solution much more quickly and easily than you had expected. I've seen shrewd negotiators make a general statement and ask if everyone agreed. Then, they'd stand up and say, "Then it's all settled. Let's get rolling." If something like that happens to you, you need to just keep your seat and say, "Wait a minute. Tell me exactly what's settled? Precisely what have we agreed to do?"

## • Answering Questions Effectively Is as Important as Asking Them with Skill

I remember something that legendary Alabama football coach Bear Bryant said after he had just set the record for winning more games than any coach in the history of the game. The reporter who was questioning him asked, "What's your secret for winning football games?"

The old Bear scratched his head and thought for a minute. Then, he said in his southern drawl, "Well, there's only two things you have to do. . . . First, you have to keep your opponent from scoring more points than you do. . . . Then, you have to score more points than your opponent does. "

Now, what the wily old coach was saying may seem obvious, but there's a great deal of wisdom in it if you're trying to ward off tough questions. Your first goal is always to answer a question in a way that doesn't allow your opponent to score a point. Then, if possible, you want to answer it in a way that scores a point for your position.

Say you've just been handed a loaded question by a tough negotiator who's trying to score a point. Maybe he has asked, "What are you going to do if we don't accept your proposal?" You may not know, and even if you do know, it would weaken your position to tell him. And you can't say, "Oh, we've got far better options than this one." If you pulled that routine, his next question would be, "Then why are you talking to us?"

So, what do you do? You could always buy some time by giving a vague answer like, "Oh, we have a number of options available." But you'd better be thinking fast, because his next question is going to be, "Like what?"

Another thing you could do would be to give him a hardball answer like, "I'd rather not say." That's a nice way of saying, "It's none of your business, bucko!"

Probably the best answer would be to look him square in the eyes, and say, "Why do you ask?" That response stops his line of questioning dead in its tracks. This approach will keep him from scoring his point, and depending on how he responds, it sets you up to score one for your position.

That's the best you can hope to do in answering a tough question. Let's look at exactly how it stops his line of questioning. Remember, he's asked you, "What are you going to do if we don't accept your proposal?" And you've responded with your own question, "Why do you ask?" That's a nice way of saying, "Look, I don't consider that a legitimate question, but if you've got a valid reason for asking it, I'll answer it." You're alerting him that you feel he's getting nosy, but that you don't want to be evasive or uncooperative if you've misread him.

So, how is he going to respond? If he says, "Well, I think I have a right to know," you can always ask another question: "Does it have some bearing on what we work out here?"

If he asks, "Why are you reluctant to answer my question?" you can come back with your own question, "Why do you want to know?"

Or suppose he says, "Oh, I was just curious." You're in a perfect position to ask a real stinger of a question: "I see, are you concerned about what I might do if we can get together?"

Just keep in mind that your first objective is always to stop a damaging line of questioning, and your second objective is to try to turn it around to your advantage. The best technique for doing that is to ask a well-chosen question of your own.

## • Don't Be Afraid to Ask

Questions open up communication and encourage people to share information. Then everyone can move from their individual positions and focus on ways they can pool their strengths to form a mutually beneficial and satisfactory agreement.

Learn to ask questions effectively, and you will have mastered one of the most powerful tools of negotiating.

## *One Last Thought . . .*

### *Practice, Timing, and Discipline: The Essentials for Success*

How do you get to Carnegie Hall? Practice, practice, practice! What is the most important thing about comedy? Timing! What is the price of success? Discipline and persistence.

Using tactics in negotiation to optimize results requires both practice and timing.

#### *Practice*

The Wince, the Red Herring, Good Guy-Bad Guy, Limited Authority, False Deadlines, Trial Balloons, and a host of other commonly used negotiation tactics are skill-based techniques. The way to perfect and preserve negotiation skills is to practice, practice, practice.

Where to practice? When working to develop the use of any particular negotiation tactics, it is essential that we practice the tactic until we are comfortable with its use.

It is rarely productive to practice during our most important transactions. We develop our tactical acumen by practicing on things that are not terribly important. Practice at the airport ticket counter, practice at the hotel registration desk, practice at the high school rummage sale, or practice at the local thrift store.

Take 20 $1 bills and be on the lookout for a swap meet, a flea market, or a rummage sale. It is fun to haggle a good deal on an old Hawaiian shirt or a desk lamp. And it is great practice!

Get your "licks" down on the small things and then you will find your conditioned response and tactical skills are ready and available when you engage in the give and take on the big deals.

### Timing

The "Dual Vision" strategy discussed in other Negotiate Like the Pros™ articles is finally implemented by using tactical techniques. It may turn out in the best deals that little or no tactics are necessary. However, when tactics are necessary to bridge the gap in the positions between parties, it is essential that we use the necessary tactics at the right time. As a rule, you should put off using tactics until we have developed clearly defined strategic objectives or measures of success. Only when positions are finely revealed does tactical negotiation become relevant. This is when our practice can really pay off!

### Discipline

Implementing a personal schedule to practice negotiation techniques is not easy. Especially as it relates to our business transactions. Over the last ten years, our Negotiate Like the Pros organization has tested numerous coaching approaches. Here is our most current regime:

- An initial one-day seminar to learn and review strategic and tactical concepts of negotiation. We use role-playing and audience participation liberally. We establish a practice schedule working on one tactic a week for eight to ten weeks.

- Next, we schedule a meeting for approximately one half day within 60 days of our initial seminar. We review our experiences in tactical practice and then identify our three most difficult challenges. We develop a game plan to meet these challenges and then go back to work.

- Another 30-day follow-up meeting is scheduled to review results. Usually our most difficult challenges are by then approachable and manageable. We can then identify our two or three most attractive business opportunities.

- A similar game plan is developed. In our final 30-day meeting, we review our experiences and compare our results.

- The four-month period described is followed up by toll-free telephone consultation through the end of a total one-year period. The results have been phenomenal!

- Our Results Plus™ plan has really allowed us to substantially impact organizations and individuals who want to achieve dramatic returns on their training dollars.

Negotiate Like the Pros is constantly on the lookout for leading organizations that are looking for real results. Perhaps your organization could be next?

· · ·

# CHAPTER FIVE

# Agree on the Ground Rules before You Jump into the Issues

IDEALLY, WE WOULD ALL COME TO THE BARGAINING TABLE WITH the intention of pooling our resources to design a solution that would provide everyone with a bigger piece of the pie. We do not, however, live in a perfect world, and we are not perfect people. When we cut through all the posturing and diplomacy, the fact is we want to get what we want. And we're not always concerned with making sure all the other people get what they want.

Sellers, for example, always want to get the highest price; buyers want to pay the lowest price. Prospective employers want to pay the minimum salary to retain a quality employee; the employee wants to earn as much as possible.

That's not to say that people don't want to be fair, but the distinction between what's actually fair and what's good for your position can sometimes be blurry when you're focusing on your goals. I have to confess that even when I tell myself that I don't want to take advantage of others, I'm not always the most objective judge of what is best for everyone involved. The problem is, we focus so steadily on our own position that we can't see the big picture clearly, even when we try. The question is, is there any hope for overcoming this weakness in human nature? The answer is yes.

## • Know What You're Negotiating

Months before leaders of the superpowers would meet, we'd start reading in newspapers and hearing on the television news what the two men will be discussing during the upcoming summit. Long before a criminal case goes to trial, both the defense and prosecuting attorneys know the charges against the defendant. Thus, they know exactly what's at stake weeks in advance of the trial. When you walk into a store and ask about a product, you and the salesperson know what the issue is: to buy or not to buy. If you ask for a raise, you and your employer know what's on the table: a fair day's work for a fair day's wages. Therefore, setting an agenda for your negotiations is a critical task. Whenever you sit down at the bargaining table, establish upfront exactly what issues you're negotiating.

## • Discuss Why You Are Meeting, and What Everyone Hopes to Gain

Discussing the goals of the meeting lets everyone know from the outset what is and what is not to be negotiated. For example, a job candidate is interviewing with a prospective employer. From the job candidate's perspective, he or she is still trying to win the job. He or she is not at the stage of negotiating terms of employment. From the employer's perspective, the candidate is the choice. Now they are only discussing the details of his or her position. The interchange between the two people gets confused when the employer starts talking about benefits and salary, and the job candidate is still trying to sell himself or herself to the company.

To establish an agenda, the employer needs to say something like, "The job is yours if you want it. We like what we see in you and feel like you can make a worthwhile contribution to this company. Let's talk about what it'll take to get you to join our team." Setting an agenda also avoids open-ended, rambling discussions that seem to make no headway. The parties involved in merger discussions might enjoy getting to know each other as they talk about the latest developments in their industry. But no one is going to benefit if they never get down to business and discuss how they can help each other. Knowing what's on the table seems like an obvious rule of negotiating effectively, but you'd be surprised how often people get into negotiations without having a clear picture of what's in it for them. If what you want is not on the bargaining table, why negotiate?

## • Capture the Power of Objective Criteria

A friend of mine, master negotiator Roger Dawson shared in his book, *You Can Get Anything You Want*, a story about a real estate agent who approached him on the edge of panic during one of his seminars. The young woman explained to Roger that she had listed a client's home for $600,000. At the time the client asked her how much commission she charged, she told him the standard fee was 6 percent. He complained that $36,000 was a lot money. She had said to him that if they had to negotiate the price down very much, she would work with him on the commission.

Well, lo and behold, the house sold in a very short time for $600,000. But guess who didn't want to pay up. The client told the real estate agent, "I've been thinking of the amount of work you had to do on the sale, and I've decided that $5,000 would be an adequate commission for you."

The dilemma the real estate agent faced, she told Roger, was that she had verbally agreed to discuss the terms of her commission. She was afraid if she insisted on the $36,000, the seller would refuse to sell the house and she would end up with nothing.

After asking her a few questions, my friend spotted the solution to her problem. Even though the two parties had not verbally agreed on a commission, the seller had signed a standard listing contract, which stated that the agent who listed and sold the home would collect a 6 percent commission. The issue of how much she would earn on the sale of the home was not negotiable. The contract, which was standard for that market, provided an impartial guideline for payment (from Roger Dawson's *You Can Get Anything You Want,* Simon & Schuster, 1986).

That contract was the objective criterion determining the outcome of the negotiations between the real estate agent and her client. Objective criteria are any fair standards, independent of the desires of either side, which set the stage for impartial negotiations.

Regardless of the real estate agent's position or the client's position, their contract established that a 6 percent commission was standard. The commission had nothing to do with how fast the house sold or how much work the agent put into it. When the client signed the contract, he agreed that the service of having his house sold was worth 6 percent of the selling price. That figure couldn't become negotiable after the service had been performed.

Remember, the perceived value of a service drops considerably after the service has been performed. When the man wanted to sell his house, the listing was worth $36,000. Once the agent found a buyer, the service wasn't worth more than $5,000. When you are negotiating, make sure you have a concrete price set before you deliver on your agreement.

### • *How to Establish Objective Criteria*
Settling negotiations by following objective criteria can often be the key to smooth bargaining. This concept is so effective that I

wish I could claim credit for it. But the kudos go to the Harvard Negotiation Project. In their book, *Getting to Yes,* project directors Roger Fisher and William Ury suggest establishing a set of objective criteria before negotiations begin, to avoid letting discussions degenerate to a battle of wills (from Roger Fisher and William Ury's *Getting to Yes,* Penguin Books, 1991, page 84).

By objective criteria, we're talking about a set of fair standards that apply equally to all sides involved in the negotiations. When you follow objective criteria, neither person gets their way based on stubbornness or on their ability to bully the other side into giving in. Good decisions are based on fair standards.

Establishing criteria, however, can be an entire process in and of itself, and it may take a little time to develop and agree on criteria. In the long run, however, it's worth it. Setting some rules can save tremendous amounts of time and energy once negotiating begins. Without fair standards to follow, people hang on to their claims, and a lot of effort is spent defending positions rather than looking for solutions. Objective criteria clear the way for seeking solutions and making decisions.

The following section describes several effective guidelines that can help you set fair standards.

**Guideline 1.** *Introduce the concept of objective criteria to the people you'll be negotiating with and explain how they will be involved in the process.* I have to warn you that every once in a while, you'll run into a problem with people who are offended by your suggestion to establish objective criteria. Some people will immediately jump to the conclusion that you're accusing them of cheating. Or they'll suspect that you're trying to slip something by them. But if you tactfully explain what you're talking about, even the reluctant type will usually agree that it's a good idea.

You can start out by saying something like, "I appreciate the opportunity to sit down and talk with you about this. I know you are very busy and I'd like to suggest a couple of things we might agree on upfront that could help us work out all the details more quickly. We may be closer together than it would seem on the surface."

Nobody can really argue with that kind of lead in. It's complimentary, optimistic, and cooperative.

**Guideline 2.** *Survey the negotiating situation.* Whenever possible, I like to know what I'm getting into before I start negotiating. So, I try to find out everything I can about what's at stake in the negotiations—for me and the people with whom I'm negotiating. And I want to know what the other side is expecting.

Have you ever heard of "discovery" in the legal sense of the word? In case you don't watch much *Court TV* and you aren't hip to lawyer lingo, discovery is where the attorneys for both the prosecution and the defense share the information they have collected on a case and plan to use during the trial. Basically, it's an effort to make sure both sides are starting on even ground. That's what I'm talking about here.

Now, I'm not suggesting that you need to give the people you'll be bargaining with an outline of your strategy. I do think it's a good idea, however, to confer with the people with whom you'll be negotiating. Talk to them about your ambitions for the negotiations, and ask them about their expectations. This is the only way you can work together to set up some rules that will ensure you'll be meeting on a level playing field.

Sometimes, depending on the seriousness of the issues, this stage of the negotiations may need to be conducted in a pre-negotiation meeting. Most of the time, however, you can just suggest that the group take some time to examine the reasons for meeting and to lay out a few ground rules before the bargaining actually starts.

**Guideline 3.** *Determine if any existing criteria or precedents apply to the issues you're negotiating.* As you move into the process of establishing objective criteria, look for existing criteria or precedents concerning the issue you're negotiating. In other words, review laws, policies, history, moral standards, or community practices, to name just a few sources, that could have an impact on your negotiations.

If you're having a house built, for example, certain building codes provide ready-made criteria for negotiating with the builder. In most states, having the wiring done by a certified electrician is non-negotiable. Therefore, the builder can't say, "For an extra $1,000, I'll hire a certified electrician." But if you want extra outlets in some rooms, you will probably have to negotiate. You'll either have to trade that for some other amenity or offer to pay more. The Blue Book value on cars is another example of an existing standard. Standards exist for just about every form of commercial negotiation you can imagine. And identifying and using existing standards can save a lot of valuable time and energy.

When the United States first began conferring with several Third World countries for the right to do deep-seabed mining in waters under their jurisdiction, the negotiating parties made little progress. India, which was representing the Third World bloc, wanted an initial fee of $60 million for each site to be explored. To put it mildly, the American companies involved in the discussions sighed in disbelief. To them, paying an initial fee—especially $60 million per site—was unreasonable.

Even if the mines produced fantastic yields, it would be years before the companies would profit from them. They stood by their claims that paying an upfront fee would place an intolerable burden on them.

Negotiations stalled until someone discovered that the Massachusetts Institute of Technology had devised a model for the costs and profits of deep-seabed mining. Once the different parties accepted that model as an objective standard, they were able to study more effectively what it would be like to mine those areas. They could see more clearly the impact of their positions. From that foundation, the parties were eventually able to reach a satisfactory agreement (from Fisher and Ury's *Getting to Yes*, page 87). Look around for any existing criteria that may set standards for your negotiations.

**Guideline 4.** *Create your own criteria for individual negotiating occasions.* Preexisting standards or criteria don't always offer the negotiating parties enough protection. Sometimes you will have to create your own, depending on the issues you're negotiating. Once everyone has agreed to discussing and establishing fair standards, you can start by explaining some of the standards you'd like to see followed. For example, if you're negotiating your salary for a new position, you might suggest such standards as:

- the average salary for that position in companies of comparable size and scope.
- your current salary level.
- the cost of living in the area where you'll be working.
- the benefits package the company is offering in addition to salary.

As you describe your suggested criteria, offer to answer any questions. Be prepared to justify your choice of standards. People can get pretty picky. A prospective employer may ask you, "Where did you get your figures on comparable salaries for similar positions?" If so, be prepared to name a credible source. And this door swings both ways. As other parties start setting guidelines, don't hesitate to ask them to explain how they arrived at their criteria. Let's say someone is selling an automobile for $5,000. If he tells you that's the Blue Book value, ask him a few questions:

- Did he adjust the figure to reflect the car's high mileage?
- What about the fact that it doesn't have air conditioning or a CD player?
- Has the car ever been in an accident, and, if so, has he adjusted the price accordingly?

Be sure that the standards someone is trying to introduce really are fair. And make sure both sides share the same interpretation of the standards.

**Guideline 5.** *Be consistent in your application of the standards.* When you're negotiating, it's tempting to use standards only for your advantage. Like I said, we all want what we want. If you abuse the standards, however, you've completely defeated the purpose of establishing objective criteria, which is to force everyone (including yourself) to play fair.

For example, let's say you and the people you're negotiating with have agreed to keep the outcome of your negotiations confidential. Don't start leaking information if you discover halfway through the process that public knowledge of your agreements could pressure the other side into making major concessions. Be fair in your application of standards. This is all a part of ethical negotiating. This brings up a good point: know what you're getting into with every standard proposed. Be sure you don't agree to a criterion that may jeopardize your position in the long run. Once you've agreed to a set of standards, however, live by the rules you've agreed on, even if it will benefit the other side.

## • Setting the Standards Pays Off

I know it seems like establishing objective criteria before you start negotiating would seem like a long, drawn-out process. But in all my years of experience, I've found without exception that it's worth the trouble.

When two parties jump into discussions over issues and proposals without discussing standards for negotiation, confusion, suspicion, and resentment can impede progress. Look, for example, at what used to happen during the Cold War when a leader from Russia would throw out a disarmament proposal through the media. Instead of U.S. negotiators welcoming a proposed cut in certain types of missiles, they usually responded very negatively. Why? Because such proposals were almost always stacked in favor of the Russian government. Of course, we did the same thing to them. But a whole different dynamic would have been put into motion if the two sides sat down and agreed on some objective criteria.

For example, representatives of the United States and Russia had agreed upfront on an objective criterion of making no public statements on subjects being negotiated before they started talks on nuclear disarmament. They were to accept the standard that says neither nation will negotiate through the media. In other words, everyone agrees to live by the same rules. That sets the stage for orderly negotiations.

That's why it's so important to set objective criteria before you begin negotiating. The criteria have to be independent of each group's will, and they have to be enforced without bias.

It's like the old adage of talking about apples and oranges. If one side is talking apples and the other is talking oranges, you'll never get together. But if you can agree on which you'll be talking about, you begin to make some real progress. In essence, setting objective criteria is agreeing on how you will negotiate.

One of the biggest reasons I'm sold on this concept is that in addition to saving you a lot of hassles once negotiation gets underway, establishing objective criteria can help you weed out people who don't want to play fair. By establishing impartial standards, you leave them with limited maneuvering room. If you insist on setting objective criteria, unscrupulous types will usually abandon the negotiations altogether, with one excuse or another. But even if they don't, you've got their hands tied.

## • What to Watch for When Setting Standards

To develop fair standards for negotiating that will guarantee an even playing field, you have to know what is "fair." In other words, be careful that you don't agree to standards that tend to give the other side an advantage. Agree only to criteria that benefit you as well as the people with whom you're negotiating.

Many times we have to negotiate with people who understand the issues we're negotiating better than we do. Maybe they've had more practice, or you're negotiating an issue on which they're experts. For example, a personnel director at a large company has probably interviewed hundreds of job candidates over the years, while you may have negotiated for a job only four or five times. The personnel director has a clearer understanding of that negotiating process. Or a salesperson may sell thousands of his or her products in a career, while you'll only buy three or four over time. Who has the most knowledge about the negotiating situation? And remember, knowledge is power. So proceed with caution when you know you will be negotiating with someone who understands the situation better than you do.

I have two suggestions for protecting yourself from people with superior knowledge in a negotiating situation. We have already discussed the first, preparation. Being prepared can make you a match for even the most qualified professionals.

Say you're going to buy a car (I keep coming back to automobile trading because it's one of those areas in our culture where a lot of bargaining takes place) and you know very little about automobiles or dealers. That makes you a sitting duck for an experienced car salesperson. Shrewd dealers love it when an elderly woman with a fat pocketbook walks in and says, "I really like that car. How much is it?" They start at the sticker price and keep adding on.

Occasionally, however, they run into an elderly woman who's been around the block a few times. She's gone to the library and read everything available on cars and car buying. She's read *Consumer Reports* annual car-rating issue and knows what mileage to expect, what the service and repair ratings are, what options are available, and which ones carry extra cost. She's bought one of those magazines or one of those computer printouts that show exactly how much markup the dealer has in every model and every option for every model. She's also arranged for her own financing and insurance, and she's written down exactly what options she wants and has set a top dollar she'll accept on the bottom line. In other words, she's prepared.

So, the salesperson walks up with a big grin on his face and says, "Good evening, ma'am. I'd sure like to put you in a sporty model like that!" She just looks at him coldly and pulls out her list. She begins, "I want this model, with only these options on it, and I'm willing to pay this much for it. Are you interested in talking?" The salesperson doesn't have a chance.

If you have the time and the initiative, you can usually find out enough information to keep from getting skinned no matter what you're negotiating. You can find out what the objective standards are for most of the items you want to purchase and for almost anything you need to negotiate.

You will, however, come into some negotiating situations where the information you need is not readily available. That's when you fall back on my second suggestion for negotiating with experts: Get your own experts. Any time you are considering a complex negotiation of any kind, it pays to get good guidance from qualified professionals at every step of the journey. Good professional advice may cost you some money upfront, but it can save you a lot of money later.

A good attorney, for example, can look at a contract and spot terms or clauses that could cost you a fortune or tie you up in lawsuits for years. Take a term like "liquidated damages," for instance. That may sound like legal mumbo-jumbo to a layperson, but a good lawyer knows that a well-worded "liquidated damages" clause can bind you to everything and the other person to almost nothing.

Anytime you're involved in any significant negotiation you don't understand completely, seek professional counsel before you make agreements of any kind—even verbal. Spoken agreements can sometimes be as binding as written contracts. If you're negotiating a complex issue, get these experts involved in the negotiating and decision-making process. Don't just have them look over the final papers.

Take the example of buying a business. A good accountant can help you understand the criteria for fixing values on such things as the owner's goodwill equity, the inventory, the fixed assets, or anything else that involves money. A competent accountant can also advise you on such things as tax consequences both you and the seller face, or what happens if you have partners, or why certain payment terms are more attractive than others. You might find out, for instance, that you can afford to offer a higher initial price if the seller will agree to better terms over the long haul.

Likewise, a good attorney can guide you in what to propose and what to accept. He or she can explain what happens if certain conditions occur, such as what happens to the rights of your heirs if you die at certain stages of a long-term agreement.

You might even want to talk to a good business broker about what kind of deal you're being offered. A community planning expert or sharp real estate broker may know about a major highway that's coming right through the highly profitable shopping center you're buying at a bargain price. Hire competent professionals early in the process. You want to make sure you're working with professionals who know and understand exactly what you're getting into. Look, I'm a lawyer and I think a pretty darn good one, but I wouldn't any more buy a franchise business without checking with an attorney who specializes in franchises than I would take off for the moon in my neighbor's homemade rocket.

Establishing objective criteria upfront is the most effective way to keep negotiations on a mature and equal level. To do that, you need to do your homework and get competent professional counsel any time you're negotiating over your head.

## *One Last Thought . . .*

### *Thrift Stores, Movies, and Mom*

#### We Negotiate Every Day

Give and take techniques abound all around us. Thrift stores, movies, and mom give us several opportunities to see everyday negotiation in action.

WINCING, LIMITED AUTHORITY, FALSE DEADLINES. Go to your local thrift store, flea market, or swap meet. Practice your negotiation techniques while buying a cheesy Hawaiian shirt. Here's how it goes:

*Merchant*: "May I help you Sir or Madam?"

*You*: "Why yes. How much is this cheesy Hawaiian shirt?"

*Merchant*: "$10."

*You*: "$10!" (a wince, followed by silence)

*Merchant*: "How about $8?"

*You*: "$8!" (another wince) "My mom said I could only spend $5 on any cheesy Hawaiian shirt I wanted." (limited authority)

*Merchant*: "$5!" (Another wince)

*You*: "Yes, and we have to leave for home in five minutes." (false deadline)

*Merchant*: "Well, okay kid, I'll let you have it for $5."

*You*: "Ah, great" you say to yourself. "I really got him."

*Merchant*: (to himself) "That's the most I've gotten for one of these dogs in months!"

## Silence In the Movies

*Weekend at Bernie's* is a great example of silence in negotiation. Although Bernie is dead, nobody seems to notice. While propped up on a sofa at a party, dead Bernie receives an offer to buy his Porsche for $35,000. Bernie is silent. Minutes later he is offered $40,000. Bernie still says nothing. Then he is offered $45,000. More silence. Even when the offer tops $55,000, Bernie still says nothing. If we acted more like Bernie, we'd put a lot more life in our negotiations.

In *Glengarry Glen Ross*, there is a scene where Al Pacino loses a sale because Kevin Spacey volunteers information in front of Pacino's client without knowing the details of the negotiations. Pacino later tells Spacey, "You never open your mouth until you know what the shot is."

Larry Winget, a Tulsa, Oklahoma-based motivational speaker, says that you never volunteer unsolicited information because it's often used in objections later.

### Mom Knows Best (Pressure Technique)

Have you ever had a pushy person try to pressure you into a quick decision on an important matter? Yielding to this kind of pressure (which is really just another false deadline) can be disastrous. Our moms knew this when we were kids. Remember when we would relentlessly badger our moms for a quick answer to a seemingly monumental problem? Mom would say, "If I have to answer you now the answer has to be no. But, if you give me some time to think about it, the answer might be yes." Smart kids are usually willing to let up a little bit in return for the potential of a positive outcome. This technique works great with pushy adults, including bosses, employees, and spouses. Try it. Mom knows best.

Keep your eyes open. Every day we are exposed to and impacted by negotiation techniques all around us. The wise negotiator is a keen observer and an aggressive adapter of effective techniques occurring in his or her presence.

· · ·

# CHAPTER SIX

# Don't Fight: Search for Solutions

I F I'VE LEARNED ANYTHING IN ALL MY YEARS OF EXPERIENCE IN negotiating, it's that getting what you want doesn't mean others can't get what they want. Expert negotiators have learned that working with other people, rather than working against them, produces better results for everyone involved.

Bargaining doesn't have to be a tug of wills. If you can learn to tug in the same direction as the people you're negotiating with, you'll be amazed at the combined strength that will result.

In their book *The Manager as Negotiator*, David A. Lax and James K. Sebenius share a story that illustrates my point beautifully. Les Winston, an entrepreneur with an extremely successful new business, was facing a serious dilemma. His former employer, Ammetal Corporation, was suing him for half of his firm's revenues earned over the past ten years.

It seems that while working for Ammetal, Les had developed a new process that could reduce the production costs for a specialty alloy. When Ammetal, which dominated the market for the alloy, told him to abandon his research, Les decided he could make it work on his own. He left the company, scraped up enough capital, and opened his own firm. Within months, he had a plant up and running. Using a process that cut production costs by 20 percent at first and eventually by 50 percent, Les's company threatened to push his former employer out of the market entirely.

Ammetal Corporation struck back with a two-blow defense. First, they announced they were building a new plant, which would be using Les's new process for the alloy. If you know anything about the metals industry, you're aware that it's almost impossible to patent a process. Their second attack was a lawsuit, which enjoined Les to stop using the process. They claimed he was violating his employment contract by using information collected while working in Ammetal labs to build his own business.

When lawyers offered him little hope of winning the case, Les turned to the prospects of negotiating a settlement to salvage his business. Les and Ammetal tossed offers and counteroffers back and forth across the table for months, but within one week of the trial date, they were still nowhere near reaching an agreement. It took an impartial negotiating advisor to ask one simple question before the bargaining began to make progress. This person asked, "What do you really want?"

Les confessed he would really like to be able to focus on research and development, and not have to hassle with raising capital and fighting off industry giants like Ammetal. He said he was working on a new and improved process for the specialty alloy that would outperform the process his plant was currently using. He went so far as to admit that he wouldn't mind working for Ammetal, except that he knew pursuing the new process on his own would earn him a fortune—even if he lost the lawsuit. Ammetal officials, who felt they had a valid claim to the process Les was using to cut them out of the market, wanted to reclaim the market.

Once the mediator understood both sides' needs and desires, he was able to lead them through steps that resulted in a satisfactory solution. Les would come back on board at Ammetal as the head of research and development, where he would be in charge of developing his promising new process. As a part of his employment package, he would receive a sizable percentage of the profit Ammetal collected as a result of the new process (from *The Manager as Negotiator* by David A. Lax and James K. Sebenius, Free Press, 1987, pages 2–5).

That way, Les got what he wanted: the ability to pursue his research and to receive profit resulting directly from his work. Ammetal got what they wanted: the lion's share of the market for the specialty alloy.

Consider for a minute what probably would have happened if the two parties had not been able to integrate their needs and find a solution. Chances are, according to the attorneys, Les would have lost had the case gone to trial. Ammetal would have won the rights to the first innovative process, built their new plant, and recaptured the number-one position in the market. But according to Les, the refined process he was developing would soon make the current process obsolete. Eventually, he would have crushed Ammetal's control of the alloy market, but only at a tremendous personal cost. He would have had to start from scratch once again, and he would have had to deal with the administrative and marketing aspect of his business, which he despised. If you want to avoid such grim scenarios, learn to approach the people you're negotiating with as partners in search of solutions, rather than as adversaries fighting to the death.

## • Moving to the Same Side of the Table

Searching for mutually beneficial solutions is, in effect, like moving to the same side of the table as your negotiating counterparts. Instead of looking at the issue from opposing viewpoints, you align your needs and desires and examine the issues as a common problem, not as a struggle over who's going to walk away with the spoils of war.

Once you've established this kind of a relationship among the people negotiating, you can work through several steps to reach a solution that meets everyone's needs.

## • *Step 1: Define the Problem or Issues that Have Brought the Parties to the Bargaining Table*

You probably learned in grade school that any successful search for a solution always begins with a well-defined problem. You have to know what the question is before you can find an answer. When negotiating, you have to define the issues to be addressed before you begin settling terms.

In the illustration involving the metallurgist and Ammetal Corporation, the two parties kept hitting a wall until they stood back and examined exactly what the issues were. Before the mediator stepped in, their focus remained on positions. Les Winston wanted the company to keep its grubby hands off his profitable operation. Ammetal Corporation wanted to recover its share of the market for the specialty alloy. Their exchanges were limited to struggles for control. The company resorted to strong-arm tactics. Their negotiations didn't move off square one until an outside observer stepped in and forced both sides to look at the real issues involved.

The first step to finding a mutually beneficial solution is to get beyond individual positions and to focus on the core issues at hand. Be willing to spend some time on this step. It's the foundation for the rest of the negotiations. When I make this point in my seminars, someone will usually speak up and say to me, "Don't you think that most people already know what the issues are?" No, not necessarily. Many times, people only think they know what the issues are. And sometimes what they consider issues are only positions.

Think about it. Most people don't focus on issues when they approach the bargaining table. They are thinking about their positions. They are thinking about what they want. To them, what they want is the issue. That's where the confusion begins. Positions are not issues.

Labor negotiations offer a good example of separating the issues from positions. Employees will tell you that the issue is more money and increased benefits. Management will tell you that holding down costs is the issue. But those aren't real issues; they are positions. The employees want increased income and benefits. The company wants to hold the line on costs. You don't get down to real issues until all parties start talking to each other about their own positions. Everyone involved must understand the negotiations from the other people's point of view.

It's not unreasonable for hard-working employees to expect raises on a regular basis. On the other hand, companies have to watch the bottom line if they plan to survive. So, the real issue isn't whether the employees get raises, but rather how we can align the legitimate concerns felt by both sides most effectively. The issue is working out a system that guarantees employees fair pay and benefits, and ensures the company's financial security.

You can see why it's important to take the time to spell out the issues, even if you think everyone understands what they are. Naturally, people see negotiations from their own perspectives. It's necessary for everyone to talk about their perceptions and assumptions.

To cut through positions, begin by discussing everyone's interests, needs, and desires. The employee representatives can talk about what they want and why they want it. Management can explain their point of view and why they feel the need not to respond to the employees' positions.

One important point to remember is that defining the problem and issues is not simply a matter of someone stating them. If you ask ten people to state a problem, you might get ten different

definitions. To be effective, this first step has to result in all parties agreeing on the definition of the problem or issue.

A good way to narrow down the scope of the issues on the
table is to ask, "What are we really trying to accomplish by negotiating?" When everybody can agree on an answer to that question, you're ready to move to the next step.

### • Step 2: Learn What People Really Want

I know it sounds like step one and step two overlap each other.
Yes, they are closely related, but they are actually quite different.
You do need to get people to talk about their positions and their
perceptions in order to accurately define the issues. But step two
is a critical transition between talking about issues and propos-
ing solutions. In step two, you try to learn what people really
want. In other words, if the problem is solved, how will all parties be better off?

For example, a brother and sister are arguing over whether
the stereo should be on or off. That is the apparent issue. The sister yells at her brother, "I have to study! That's more important
than you listening to your stupid Creed CD! So turn it off!"

The brother shouts back, "Oh yeah? You don't have to study
in the den! You can go to your bedroom!" And back and forth
they go until Dad steps in. After listening to both sides of the
argument, he walks over to the stereo cabinet, pulls out a head-
set, and hands it to his son. Argument settled. It's really just
common sense. The dad had to find out exactly what each kid
wanted before he could see what kind of compromise they both
could accept.

Step one was to define the issue—how can two people with
conflicting interests share a common space? And step two was
identifying the real desires of both. The main reason I have step
two as a separate component from step one is to help you realize that getting down to interests is not as simple as asking people what they want.

The girl probably would have told her father that she wanted
the stereo turned off so she could study. Her brother would have

repeated that she could go to her bedroom. But the sister didn't really want to stop her brother from listening to his music, even if she called it stupid. She just didn't want the noise to interfere with her studying. Conversely, the brother wasn't bent on making it impossible for his sister to study, or even making her study somewhere else. After listening to them, the father could see a solution that neither of them had even thought of. We need to learn to do the same thing in all our negotiations.

Effective questioning skills are vital for completing step two successfully. You have to ask the right questions to get people to talk about more than their positions. Sometimes we're so emotional about our positions that we overlook what we really want.

As I showed you earlier, asking the right questions can peel away the layers of mistrust and cut through the misperceptions and confusion that tend to muddy the waters of negotiation.

## • Step 3: Design Creative Options that Will Meet Everyone's Needs

I've established that one of the most expensive mistakes you can make in negotiating is to assume that the only option is for one side or the other to profit. Any student of famous negotiations throughout history can tell you that the most successful arrangements have entailed authoring agreements that went beyond exchanging concessions for gains.

What I like about this third step is that if you've done a good job with the first two steps, most people are extremely cooperative by the time you get to this stage. They've worked their way through their misperceptions and differences, and everyone sees themselves sharing a common goal. That goal is to reach a mutually beneficial and satisfactory agreement. They have come around to the same side of the bargaining table and they perceive the problems as the enemy, not each other. They form a common bond in their search for a mutually satisfying agreement, which is the essence of my negotiating strategy. We all know that people can accomplish so much more if they're willing to lower their guard just a little and look for their similarities with others. That's much more productive than focusing on differences.

Scientific studies have repeatedly shown that stress blocks creativity, although a certain amount of tension can actually be good because it keeps all the participants on their toes. There's always going to be some tension in any significant negotiation, but the key is to keep the tension at the right level. It's a little like a string on a violin. If it's too loose, it squawks like crazy. If you twist it one turn too tightly, it snaps. But if that string has just the right tension on it, it produces magnificent musical tones, at just the right pitch.

So if you want creativity to flourish in your negotiations, look for the right balance between too much tension and too relaxed an atmosphere.

Although I talk about the importance of generating creative ideas, I have to confess there really is no plan or set of steps you can follow to unlock your creative energies. Different environments and conditions stimulate people, so I don't recommend trying to get people to follow any sort of rigid system for inspiring creativity. But I can suggest a few ideas to keep in mind when you're trying to develop creative options for settling issues.

Many people find brainstorming sessions helpful in the early stages of the search for a solution. The best way to do that is to get together with the people you're negotiating with and start batting around ideas. The basic purpose of brainstorming is to throw out all kinds of ideas, no matter how wild they are. Don't criticize ideas, or the people who suggest them, during this stage of the creative process. Criticism poisons creativity, especially if it's directed at an individual.

Be open minded. Don't be afraid to voice off-the-wall suggestions, and don't attack other people for their ideas. The only way brainstorming will work is if everyone shares their ideas and invites others to dream up possible solutions. Let me warn you that brainstorming can take a lot of time, but it's well worth it. Creative solutions are not the obvious solutions. That's what makes them creative. And most of us don't do a lot of creative thinking. I don't mean that as an accusation or criticism, but it's true. We've had our creativity socialized out of us. So it takes time and effort to shake the alternative solutions free from the recesses of our rusty minds.

Now don't expect brainstorming to produce a plethora of feasible solutions, because it almost never does. That's not its purpose. Brainstorming is a method of opening up the flood-gates of creativity. You're just supposed to let the ideas flow uncontrolled. It's a way of looking at the same facts and seeing something different.

You will get the results you're looking for once you have a fair number of ideas. Start sifting through them and looking for the workable parts. Sometimes, you can combine parts of different ideas to come up with one solid plan. Or maybe some of the original ideas just need a little fine tuning, which is the next stage of searching for creative options. You piece together feasible ideas that are acceptable to everyone involved.

Once you've got some solid ideas in hand, you're practically home free. Since everyone was involved in generating the ideas, they're more likely to accept at least some of the proposals presented. People don't usually disagree with their own ideas. Not only that, people usually follow through on the plans they helped to create so you can count on people to hold up their end of the bargain. They feel a sense of ownership for the agreement. They should; they designed it!

## • Finalize and Clarify

Making sure people's perceptions match is just as crucial in the final stages of negotiation as it is throughout the process. I can't tell you how many seemingly productive negotiations have disintegrated because the people involved misunderstood the terms of the agreement.

For example, a customer calls a sales representative one Wednesday morning: "Where are those bearings I ordered? They were supposed to arrive by 9 A.M. It's noon, and they're not here.

If we don't have them by 2 P.M., we have to shut down our production. The main reason I switched to your company was because you said your shipping department had less than a 1 percent missed deliveries rate. The deal is off, Clark. I'm calling our old supplier." Blam, he slams down the receiver. What happened? Clark misunderstood the customer when they were filling out the final details on the sales contract. His records show the bearings were to be delivered the following Wednesday. He didn't know how it happened, but somehow the lines of communication got crossed. He was faced with losing a potentially lucrative account and suffering terminal damage to his reputation.

Scenes like this one happen all the time. We've all done it, and we've all been the victims of misunderstandings. The only solution is to clarify, clarify, clarify. Once you find a solution and you've reached an agreement, make sure all parties understand the details of the agreement and that they understand what is expected of them. In other words, clarify the details of the commitment. Don't hesitate to restate explicitly the details of the arrangement. For example, you can say, "Just to be sure we all understand the solution and what's expected, let me recap our agreement." Then cover every detail of the contract. Depending on the level of the negotiations, it's not a bad idea to put everything in writing.

If a negotiation doesn't result in a signed contract, write a letter to the people you were bargaining with that restates your agreement explicitly and outlines what is expected of everyone. That way, you will have a written record of everyone's commitment. If anyone disagrees with your interpretation of the agreement, they can respond to your letter, which I suggest you send no later than the day after the negotiations. Don't let the fruits of your negotiating labor evaporate because of misunderstandings or misconceptions. Clarify and finalize all agreements.

## • Follow Through

I have an assignment for you. Look through some books on the history of the world, and count the number of treaties that have been blown away like dry leaves because one or more of the parties involved failed to follow through. Don't be surprised by the high number.

It doesn't matter how brilliant your solutions are if one person fails to follow through on his or her commitments. As I said earlier, complete follow-through is an integral part of negotiating. One misstep can negate all your negotiating efforts.

Follow-through is simple: It means that you do what you said you would when you said you would do it in the manner you said you would do it. If, for some reason, you are unable to follow through on an item or detail, notify the people involved and work out an alternative agreement. You probably would expect the same courtesy from the people you deal with, right?

## • High Standards Pay Off

When examined under the harsh lights of reality, some of the principles we've talked about in this chapter probably sound a little like Pollyanna to you. I know, because I've heard that comment in my seminars. After all, you might say, even if you know that working with, rather than against, negotiating counterparts is more productive how do you convince the people with whom you're negotiating?

First, accept the fact that not everybody is going to cooperate. Some people are just not willing to negotiate fairly. They want to get everything they can, and they don't care what they have to do to get it. With these people, the best you can hope to do is to protect yourself. Look out for your own skin, and don't get suckered in by their tactics.

However, most people aren't like that. I've always found that if I play fair with others, most of them will play fair with me. Sure, they want to get the best deal they can get. They don't have any ill will toward the people they're negotiating with, but they don't want to walk away from the bargaining table empty-handed.

I'd say that's the category in which you and I, and about 6.4 billion other people on this planet, fit. We don't want to be adversaries; all we want is to come out of every negotiation with as good a bargain as we can get. So getting people to cooperate is not as difficult as it might seem. It all goes back to overcoming those myths of negotiation I talked about earlier. People don't necessarily want to get into a struggle over positions. They simply want what they want. And that is the key.

Don't forget why people negotiate in the first place. They want or need something the other party has. If they don't, you can't even get them to start the negotiating process. People only negotiate when they feel a need or desire for something. Getting people to work together on designing solutions is simply a matter of showing the people you're negotiating with that working together will move them closer to getting what they want.

## One Last Thought . . .

## World Class Negotiation: Working Door-to-Door in the Global Village

Sydney, Australia was the destination. Quantas Flight AF008 (LAX to Sydney nonstop) was the particular flight. My seat assignment was 58H in Economy. Yes, Economy happens. I'd tried all my best techniques with the counter attendant but to no avail. Wearing a suit to appear the perfect upgrade candidate, smiling, commiserating with her obviously heavy workload, volunteering to move up to business or first class to help better distribute weight throughout the aircraft. Nothing worked.

No one gets what they want every time—even Mr. Negotiator. However, the real lesson here is never give up. Though I didn't obtain the obvious objective of an upgrade, the counter attendant did, however, block the seat between myself and the fellow next to me. And it was a full flight.

Every adversity offers an equal or greater opportunity! The reputation of this mantra helped me to accept my fate—Seat H, Row 58 in Economy. I exchanged polite introductions with my fellow occupant (Bob) of Row 58 (right side Economy on a 747–400 aircraft). Through three meal services, two bar services, and four feature films, we became better acquainted.

As It turns out, Bob was a writer from *The New York Times* traveling through Sydney to Papua, New Guinea. His assignment was to write an article on travel and leisure. By exchanging information and references, Bob and I made a great deal on our (LawTalk is our company) new legal lifestyle magazine. In return, I provided him with suggestions on how to navigate through Customs and Immigration in Sydney, and what sights to see before he traveled north to the jungle. We negotiate every day. And we never know when the use of our give-and-take talents will result in an unforeseen long-term benefit.

The Southern Cross Hotel in Sydney is a great place. The staff at the Southern Cross is so congenial that I choose to stay there each time I travel to Sydney. "This is a suite, isn't it?" (I received a suite for the same price as a regular room.) Always ask for an upgrade when you book your hotel reservation and again when you check in.

After a week of heavy negotiation on several business deals, it was time to go home. Seat 58H was bad enough. On my return flight, I convinced the counter attendant to allocate me seat 48H (bulkhead exit row). More leg room! (I thought.) Unfortunately, 48H is also the area where people congregate waiting for an opportunity to use the bathroom. "Be careful what you ask for because you just might get it!"

was my new mantra. Remember, world-class negotiation techniques are powerful tools but we should always keep in mind that we use these techniques door-to-door—one person at a time.

· · ·

# CHAPTER SEVEN

# Mastering Basic Negotiating Tactics

S AY THE WORD "TACTICS" WHEN YOU'RE TALKING ABOUT NEGO-
tiating, and people automatically assume you're giving
them advice on how to trick someone into making a mistake at the bargaining table. Herb Cohen, author of *You
Can Negotiate Anything*, (Bantam, 1982, page 108) says, "To
achieve a collaborative result in a competitive environment, you have to play the game." In other words, using
so-called "negotiating tactics" doesn't automatically mean
you are trying to manipulate or trick others.

Most of us enter negotiations knowing that the other
side is going to use certain maneuvers to tip the scales in
their favor. Prospective employers will offer you less than

they are willing to pay to give themselves negotiating room. A buyer will act shocked at a seller's stated price, no matter how reasonable it is, to pressure that person into lowering it. We all do it, but this doesn't mean that we're crooks, unwilling to negotiate fair terms. You can use tactics, and still maintain your negotiations on an honest and mature level. Tactics, as Herb Cohen says, are just a part of the game.

Now, I have to admit there are some tactics that I avoid using. I think they're sleazy and designed to rip people off. But you'd better be able to recognize them, if for no other reason than to prevent people from using them against you.

## • Fourteen Common Negotiating Tactics

I probably don't have to tell you that I don't advocate the use of tactics to take advantage of the people with whom you're negotiating. I believe that most tactics, if used judiciously, are simply tools that can expedite the negotiating process.

Tactics serve several purposes. They help you get down to the real issues being debated at the negotiating table. They can break down stalemates. And they can help you spot and protect yourself from unscrupulous negotiators.

Take a look at the 14 most common negotiating tactics and ways you can use—and deflect—them to get what you want at the negotiating table.

### • *Tactic 1: The Wince*

The wince, also known as the flinch, is any overt negative reaction to someone's offer. In other words, you act stunned when the party you're negotiating with names their terms. Wincing at the right times can save you thousands of dollars over the years.

Here's how it works: Say you go to buy a car. You're looking at a convertible sports coupe sparkling under the showroom lights. The salesperson can smell your hunger and saunters up to you. He says something like, "Isn't she a beaut? And, for only $35,000, you can drive her home today."

You say, "$35,000, huh? That's not as bad as I expected."

So the salesperson says, "Yeah, and even after you add options and dealer prep charges, you're still not going to pay much more than $40,000."

You say, "That sounds reasonable." You can bet the salesperson is probably drooling at this point. So, he says, "I can also give you a deal on our extended warranty. For a $1,000 extra, you'll have bumper-to-bumper protection for six years or 60,000 miles."

You then say, "Well, if I'm investing that much money to begin with, I might as well have the best warranty available." And on and on it goes. The salesperson will keep jacking up the price as long as you keep agreeing. The wince is your best defense against this kind of massacre.

No matter what price or terms someone gives you, act shocked, even appalled. You might say, "*$35,000!* You've got to be kidding!" You could even start to turn away from the vehicle. To keep the salesperson interested, you might want to say something like, "I knew I'd have to spend a little extra for a nice sports car, but that's ridiculous."

What do you think the salesperson is going to do ? Is he going to start adding on more features at extra cost? No, he's going to start talking to you about ways you can cut the cost of the car. He might say, "Of course, $35,000 is the sticker price. We're allowed some room for negotiation. Do you have a trade-in?"

And on and on that goes, with you in the driver's seat.

A wince tells the person you're dealing with that you have your limits. There's nothing dishonest or under-handed about that. Most of the people I know, even those who are well off, have their limits. On negotiable items, the price is marked up so the salespeople have some negotiating room. If a wince helps you get a better price, don't worry about the salesperson. He or she is not going to suffer.

Of course, you will not always be the wincer. Sometimes, you will be the wincee. So what can you do when your negotiating counterpart chokes for air when you name your price? Fall back on one of the strongest tools in negotiating, which is Tactic 2.

### • *Tactic 2: Silence*

Silence is more than golden; it is power. If you don't like what someone has said, or if you've just made an offer and you're waiting for a response, silence can be your best friend. Most people can't stand dead air time. They become uncomfortable if there's no conversation filling the void between you and them. If you just sit back and wait, almost without fail, the other person will start whittling his or her position. It's the "next-person-who-speaks-loses" syndrome. If, after you've named your terms, the other side just stares at you in disbelief, look right back at them. Don't start chiseling away at your price. Just let the silence do your talking for you. Even if someone tries to fight your silence with silence, don't give in. Just keep repeating in your head: "He who speaks first comes in last. He who speaks first comes in last."

Occasionally you will run into someone who's as good at silence as you are, and you both end up just sitting like mutes. I know you can feel as if you're going to burst if you don't say something. In that case, you're allowed to talk. Simply restate your offer. Don't make suggestions. Just repeat exactly what you said before the silence fell over the meeting. That maneuver forces the person or people you're negotiating with to respond. Usually they will respond with a concession.

The judicious use of silence can be one of your strongest negotiating tools.

### • *Tactic 3: The Good Guy/Bad Guy Routine*

You've probably seen this tactic in detective movies. This is the technique where you have two detectives in a room working over some guy who's been arrested. One person seems to be unreasonable and inflexible. He may be pacing up and down the room, threatening to throw the book at the person being interrogated. He may even storm out of the room. The other detective tries to make it look like he or she is on the side of the suspect and might be able to help. Like most tactics, this one is designed to get you to make concessions without the other party making any in return. You'll find this little dance going on in real estate all the time. The agent will try to make you think it's the seller who's not interested in lowering the price. The agent wants you to see him or her as an ally, not someone who's working for the other side.

Here's an example of how their routine usually works: After you've made an offer on a house, the real estate agent will come back to you with something like, "The sellers have rejected your offer. I wish I could convince them to lower their price a little, but they're determined. I'd really hate for you to lose this house. I know your heart is set on it. Do you think we could work something out?" Of course, they don't want you to lose the house. They want to make a sale. But they also want to make it at the highest price possible. They just want you to think that they want to bring the cost down. They don't. Make no mistake about it. Real estate agents always work for the seller. The money is in listing and selling houses. And the more they can sell a house for, the more money they will make.

The best response to this tactic is to ignore it. Recognize it for what it is, but don't play along with it. Don't let the good guy get next to you, and don't let him or her influence your decision. Just remember, that person is not your friend or ally.

Sometimes the good guy will start to pressure you in a non-threatening way. If that happens, you might find it effective to call him or her on it. You can say, "Hey, I know what's going on here, and I'm not falling for it." Of course, whether you call your negotiating counterpart's hand depends on individual situations. I make it a habit to avoid accusing people of trying to manipulate me if I believe I can still profit from our negotiations. Most often the best technique is to let them play their little game while you watch out for your interests.

## • Tactic 4: Limited Authority

Limited authority is a variation of the good guy/bad guy routine. Instead of two people working you over, you are dealing with one person who tells you that he or she must OK any deals with a—you guessed it—"higher authority." Sometimes there really is a higher authority lurking in a top-floor office somewhere. Other times, that authority is only a figment of the person's imagination, hatched to give him or her an edge in negotiations.

Say an employee asks his boss for a raise. His boss tells him, "Well, your work has been good, and I appreciate your dedication, but you know I don't make those decisions. I'll have to check with Ms. Hampton." That's the beauty of the limited authority technique. What has the boss done? He has basically said, "I can't negotiate this with you. If you want to tell me your side of the story, I'll go talk to Ms. Hampton." That employer is getting the employee to give up a lot of information without giving any in return. The employee might as well be talking to a tape recorder. And that's not negotiation.

The best way to handle this tactic when someone tries it on you is to say, "OK, I understand that you can't make a decision. But I would feel more comfortable talking directly with Ms. Hampton. Maybe the three of us could meet one day this week." Immediately the other person knows that you're not going to rollover and play dead. Regardless of whether the higher authority is a real person or some character conjured up to obstruct fair negotiations, you maintain control in the bargaining. You're saying, "I can live with that. Just let me know who I need to talk to."

There are two keys to breaking down the facade of limited authority. First, you need to find out who the real decision maker is. In other words, you need to pin down who you need to talk with to get action, whether it's the person who's hiding behind limited authority or some individual up the ladder somewhere. If at all possible, you need to negotiate directly with the person or people who can give you the decision you want.

Secondly, you need to apply as much pressure as you can without making threats you don't intend to carry out. Just because someone tells you, "It's out of my hands," don't automatically assume it's true. Test the limits of that person's authority. It may simply be a tactic to get you to back away. If you keep coming, you may get exactly what you want.

## • *Tactic 5: The Red Herring*

The name of this tactic comes from old English fox hunting competitions. One team would sometimes drag a smelly fish across the path of the fox to confuse the other team's dogs and make them lose the trail. People rarely bring smelly fish into negotiating rooms, but they are not above doing whatever it takes to distract the people they're negotiating with from the main issues on the table.

Effective and ethical negotiators agree almost without exception that the red herring is the sleaziest of techniques. I'm not in favor of using it, except in rare cases. For example, one of my partners, a divorce lawyer, was representing a woman who was going through a bitter settlement battle with her estranged husband. As a criminal lawyer, I can tell you that I would rather defend an axe murderer than handle a divorce.

Anyway, the husband was doing everything possible to make life miserable for my partner's client. Everything was settled except one issue—the couple's art collection. They had invested in some valuable art pieces during the eight years of their marriage, and that collection was about the only thing the woman was interested in keeping.

Naturally, the husband decided that he couldn't live without the art collection. So my partner decided the time had come to get the man's attention off the art collection. Actually, she just narrowed the focus a little. She had her client select her least favorite pieces. My partner then approached the woman's husband and told him that, his ex-wife wanted only those three pieces.

Guess what happened? The husband immediately claimed those three as his favorites. He went on to say that there was no way he was going to let his wife have them. My partner, rubbing the herring into the ground for good measure, argued vehemently with the husband. Finally, she met with the husband one more time. She said to him, "It makes her sick, but your wife has agreed that you can keep those three pieces, if she can have the rest of the collection." Puffed up with self-satisfaction, the husband agreed to her terms.

If you find yourself a victim of the red herring, you need to have a defense prepared. The first thing you need to do is recognize it for what it is.

Usually, a red herring is some highly emotional issue that has no real substance to it. Its purpose is to draw attention away from much more important matters. Sometimes, it's used as a delay tactic to keep the negotiations bogged down on minor issues until circumstances change and tilt the balance of power to the stalling side. Occasionally, it's used like smoke and mirrors to keep you from noticing a bit of information that would turn you off completely to a proposed deal. Most often, it is used to trick you out of money.

Regardless of how it's used against you, always keep your eyes on the most important issues you are negotiating. If you suspect that someone is using a red herring against you, pull out the old set-aside trick. Simply say, "Apparently, we're not getting anywhere on this issue. Set it aside for now and work out all the other details. If we get everything else settled, we can always come back to this later."

If you are bogged down on a minor issue, and your negotiating counterparts insist on settling it before they'll even talk about any other issue, you are probably dealing with a red herring tactic. In that case, you'd better proceed with extreme caution.

## • Tactic 6: The Trial Balloon
Trial balloons are questions designed to help you assess your negotiating counterpart's position without giving any clues about your plans. Here are a few sample trial balloons:

- "Would you consider coming to work for us on a temporary basis?"

- "How do you feel about working on straight commission?"
- "Have you ever thought about moving into management?"

The nice thing about trial balloons is that they are not really offers. They help you get information without making a commitment.

The answers you get in response to trial balloons can give you an idea of where you stand at any given moment, and they can tell you where the other party's interests lie. Trial balloons also let you know how serious the other people are about negotiating an agreement. You find out if they are flexible and willing to work things out or if they are rigid in their positions.

Obviously, trial balloons seem less attractive when you're on the receiving end. They can put you in a tough position if you feel compelled to answer them thoroughly. Personally, I think you should always try to answer trial-balloon questions with another question that will give you an idea of why your counterpart is sending it up in the first place. For example, if someone asks, "Would you consider financing the house yourself?" respond, "Well, if I did consider financing it myself, what would your offer be?" Always try to get the ball back in their court. Here's a little bonus tip: Always try to get the other person to make the first move.

## • Tactic 7: Lowballing

Lowballing is just the opposite of the trial balloon. Instead of trying to get you to make the first offer, the other side opens with a fantastic offer. Once you agree to the basic offer, then they start hitting you with a bunch of "by the ways."

For example, you see an ad for a computer with a price that is about a third less than other stores are asking for the same machine. You go in and the salesperson gets you to commit to buying the machine at the low price and you think you have a bargain. Then, he starts saying, "Oh, by the way, we're going to have to upgrade the memory before it will run your software.

That'll be $600. You'll need a monitor at $300. And you've got to have a monitor card. Those run $200." By the time all the necessary options are added, at inflated prices, you'll end up paying more for your computer than you would at a store that advertises higher prices.

### • Tactic 8: The Bait and Switch

The bait-and-switch tactic is closely related to lowballing. This is the age-old scenario of where you go into a store looking for an item that's been advertised at a ridiculously low price, and the salesperson says, "Gee, I'm sorry. We just sold the last one of those. But we do have this much better model at a very good price."

The people who use this approach try to attract you with one offer and then hook you with another. Watch out. You will almost always get burned in this game. If the people using it were able to offer a genuinely good deal, they wouldn't be resorting to the bait and switch.

### • Tactic 9: Outrageous Behavior

Outrageous behavior is any form of conduct—usually considered socially unacceptable—with the purpose of forcing the other side to make a move. A fit of anger. A burst of tears. You read in the newspapers all the time about these shenanigans during labor negotiations. A union representative who doesn't like something a company person says jumps up and turns over the table. Or management gets fed up with what they consider unreasonable demands and someone tears up the contract and throws it in the air outside the building where the negotiations are being held, such as in front of a horde of media people.

The goal of these outbursts is to rattle the other people involved in the negotiations. Most of us don't like volatile or emotional confrontations, and we'll do whatever it takes to avoid them. Richard Nixon used this tactic with tremendous effect toward the end of the Vietnam War. By mining Haiphong's harbor, threatening to bomb and misinforming the North

Vietnamese intelligence that he was willing to resort to low-yield nuclear weapons to end the conflict, Nixon painted himself as a half-crazed commander who wanted to end the war, no matter what the cost.

Retrospective reports revealed that Nixon never seriously considered using nuclear weapons. The president was hoping his outrageous behavior would force the other side to come to the bargaining table. The strategy was beginning to work when the Nixon administration started to crumble.

The most effective response to outrageous behavior is no response. Just wait for the gusts of anger or emotion to die down before reacting. Once again, silence can be your strongest defense against emotional outbursts. No matter what happens, don't respond emotionally. Letting emotions take over in negotiations is asking for disaster. If you respond emotionally, you will probably say and do things you regret. You might make concessions just to end the tirade. Or you may flush negotiations right down the drain because you end up punching the other person in the face. Believe me, I've seen it happen. No matter what the other side says to you, no matter what they do, short of physically attacking you, keep your emotions in check. Remaining calm keeps you in control of the negotiating situation. It's like when a child throws a temper tantrum. The best way to respond is to ignore it. Let the people having a fit wear themselves out and calm down, but don't join in the commotion.

### • *Tactic 10: The Written Word*
Terms that are laid out in black and white seem nonnegotiable. Lease agreements, loan forms, or prices most of us believe are chiseled in stone when they are presented to us on paper are some examples.

Have you rented any property, a house, or apartment lately? If so, you probably remember signing a lease agreement. Did you question anything on that contract? How many people do you think question that agreement? How many people object to it because it completely negates all the tenants' rights? Almost no one questions it. Why? Because the agreement is written in legalese. It's on official-looking paper. It's packaged in such a way that it makes people think it's law. That's a perfect illustration of the power of the written word. For some reason, most of us believe that if it's in writing, we can't question it. Or we think that the other person either isn't going to change the terms, or doesn't have the power to make any changes.

The best defense against this tactic is simple—question everything. Certainly, you'll run into situations where the form is standard or the person you're dealing with doesn't have the authority to negotiate with you. But it won't hurt to ask a few questions or to try to change the terms so they meet your needs as well. You'd be surprised how many contracts can be negotiated if you challenge them.

The worst thing that can happen is that the person or people will tell you "no." In that case, you need to ask yourself two questions before you sign or agree to anything:

1. How badly do I want or need this (whatever it is you're negotiating)?
2. How serious are the concessions I'll have to make if I can't negotiate the issues that concern me?

In other words, what are your options? Are you desperate? Do you need to go along with the other side and accept their written terms? And if you do accept them, are you going to suffer? Every case will be unique, but remember—you don't have to follow someone else's rules just because they've shoved a piece of paper in front of you.

## • *Tactic 11: The Vise*

The vise tactic is also known as the squeeze, and it usually starts with a phrase like, "You'll have to do better than that."

A man walks into an appliance store looking for a refrigerator. After finding one that seems to suit his needs, the salesperson says, "This one, with an automatic ice maker included, is only $1,500." The customer shakes his head and says, "Oh, you'll have to do better than that."

That pressures the salesperson to start shaving the price. He might respond by saying, "Well, we normally have a $40 delivery fee. But, if you buy today, I can waive that charge." The customer just looks at him and says, "Well, I appreciate that, but I was planning on picking it up myself. So, you'll still need to adjust that price some."

This tactic is called the vise because the person using it keeps pushing to get the other party to name their bottom line. The vise works by making its victims think they will have to make all the concessions if the deal is going to go through. The vise also works for the user by allowing him or her to make demands without naming a price or terms.

You can escape the vise when it is used on you. As soon as someone says to you, "You'll have to do better than that," you simply say, "Oh? How much better will I have to do?" That question forces the person to commit to at least a ballpark figure. That way, you're not as likely to cut your own throat trying to guess what's "better."

If that doesn't work, another effective counter tactic you can use to break the vise is to simply ask, "Are you really serious about this?" That question implies that you think the person is just stringing you along and wasting your time. After about three or four you'll-have-to-do-better-than-thats, look the person straight in the eye and ask, "Are you really serious about this?" Yes, this is a blunt measure, but it usually gets things moving. If not, the people using the vise are not interested in negotiating ethically and you're better off walking away from the bargaining table.

## • Tactic 12: The Trade-Off

The trade-off is probably the most above-board negotiating tactic in the whole bag of tricks people carry with them into the bargaining arena. The trade-off is simply swapping concessions at the bargaining table until everyone agrees with the terms. Trade-off is actually negotiating lingo for compromise.

A classic example of a trade-off is when two people state their terms and end up splitting the difference. The seller asks

$10,000 for an item. The buyer offers $8,000. Eventually they settle on $9,000. Of course, it can get more involved than that,
depending on the seriousness of the issue you're negotiating.

One rule about trade-offs: Never make a concession without
getting one in return. For instance, the people you're buying a
house from want to stay in the house two weeks past the closing
date. In addition to charging them standard rent, ask them to
pick up the closing costs. Or ask them to make repairs that you
had planned to attend to after they moved out. Be sure you get
fair compensation in return for your inconvenience.

### • *Tactic 13: The Nibble*

I also call this the "oh-by-the-way" technique. You've already
got a signed contract or a done deal, and the other side says,
"Oh, by the way, this price includes installation, doesn't it?" Or
they add, "Oh, by the way, we'll need this shipment delivered by
tomorrow afternoon." Nibblers try to get something for nothing
by acting like they are asking for nothing. They wait for the
terms of your agreement to be settled, then they start adding
"minor" requests or adjustments to the deal.

Watch out for nibbling, because it can be one of the most dev-
astating negotiating tactics. One reason is that the nibbles usually
seem so minor that you will readily agree to them. Let's say
you're just about ready to sign a closing agreement on your
house, and the buyer says, "Oh, by the way, you will have those
two dead trees in the backyard removed before we move in,
won't you?" You're anxious to get out from under your house
payment, so you agree. You think, "What's a couple of old dead
trees? No big deal."

Another reason nibbles can be so dangerous is that people
who know what they are doing usually keep nibbling until you're
chewed down to the bone. After you've agreed to removing the
trees, the other side will talk about another issue for a while. Then,
with pen poised over the signature line, they look up and say,
"This sale does include having a professional housekeeping service clean up the house before we move in, doesn't it?"

The danger with nibbling is that you are especially vulnerable right as an agreement is being cinched. You don't want to lose the deal. You figure these little nibbles are insignificant—after all, the important issues have been worked out, and that's what matters, right? Wrong. A bunch of little concessions can eat you alive. Just stick to the rule that you never make concessions without getting something in return.

Propose trade-offs for every request a party makes as you are closing a deal. You can say, "We don't mind taking care of the trees. But you do realize that will affect our price?" Or, "We can bring in a professional housekeeping service, but that will delay your move by at least a week."

Don't let people take advantage of you.

## • Tactic 14: Funny Money

Say you're shopping for a home computer system. The salesperson at the last shop you stop in asks you what else you've seen and what's impressed you most. You tell her that you like her company's equipment, but you can get a better price at a store across town.

After you tell the salesperson that it's about a $2,500 difference, she says, "I can see why that lump sum is putting you off, but, you know, it's not really that big of a difference." She goes on to explain that if you divide that difference over the amount of time that you're planning to finance your purchase, you're actually only paying 50 cents more per day. She might even go so far as to say, "Why, you probably spend that much on your coffee break."

Don't buy it—$2,500 is $2,500, unless you adapt it to a loan agreement that turns into more than $2,500. Have you ever seen those television commercials for aluminum siding? They give you the pitch, "For only $59 a month, you can give your home that fresh new look that only quality siding can give it!" They don't tell you that you'll be shelling out that payment for 1,200 months.

Money is money, no matter how you divide it. If you don't feel comfortable with a lump sum, don't get suckered in by the funny-money figure.

## • The Dynamics of Tactics

Some people rush in to the negotiating situation like it's a battle and start firing off tactics indiscriminately. They don't consider the impact the tactics will have on the people they're negotiating with. All they know is that these tactics have worked for others for years, so they're going to work for them.

Some people absolutely refuse to use tactics, no matter how innocent the tactic itself, or how brutal the people with whom they are negotiating. They just keep restating their position and never join in the game of negotiation.

I believe there's a happy medium between these two extremes. Certainly not every tactic works in every situation with every person. But there are times when many of these tactics can expedite the negotiating process without compromising your commitment to ethical proceedings. Choosing the right tactics and the right time to use them is crucial to effective negotiations. For example, I think the wince is appropriate any time I'm working with another professional negotiator or salesperson. It's all a part of the game, and I know professionals have built what I call a "wince buffer" into their price and terms. They've padded their offer knowing full well that most people will grab their chests in shock when they hear the proposal. I wouldn't use that tactic, however, when hiring a neighborhood kid to mow my lawn unless I thought the little rascal was a shrewd negotiator. I can't give you any foolproof guidelines on when to use which tactics. Through my examples, I've shown you ways to use and deflect tactics more effectively, but knowing exactly when to use what tactics comes only with experience and with the understanding that every negotiating situation is different.

Decide what tactics will work effectively for you as you get into each negotiating situation. Practicing good human relations—that is, dealing fairly and honestly with people—is about the most powerful tactic I know. It may sound old fashioned, but it still works best in the long haul. Don't approach negotiations as nothing more than an exchange of tactics and counterattacks. Build a strategy that focuses on working out the best agreement for everyone involved. Use and respond to tactics as only some of the steps of the process.

## One Last Thought . . .

### Let's Just Split it Down the Middle

#### Everybody's Heard of It

If there's one thing we all know about negotiation it's the "split it down the middle" (SIDTM) technique. You're very close on the purchase of your first car (in my case, a 1956 Thunderbird in 1966), the difference between what the seller is asking ($850 for the T-bird) and what the buyer is offering ($750 is what I'd offered), and so one party offers and the other party accepts an inducement to "split it down the middle."

#### Everybody's Used It

In the realm of give and take it's almost genetic. On every continent, in every culture, and in every kind of transaction the SIDTM technique is known and practiced.

#### What Makes it Attractive?

Why does SIDTM work? What dimensions of this technique cause it to be so universally embraced? Fairness is first. The element of fairness in SIDTM is extant in the fact that both parties give and both parties get something. The SIDTM compromise works for both parties. We obtain a concession, we grant a concession. What could be more fair?

Time savings is also an important and valuable consideration in SIDTM. We all have an internal time clock running within our gut. There comes a juncture in many negotiations when we conclude the expenditure of additional time on a particular transaction becomes counterproductive. Let's just "split it down the middle and get this thing over with!" Finally, SIDTM is the transition from negotiation to performance. The closure provided allows us to begin to receive the benefit of our bargains.

### It's a Great Tactic, but an Awful Strategy

This wonderful tactic, however, can lead us into an awful strategy. Why? It seems as though the combination of an almost universal death of negotiation training and the almost universal knowledge of SIDTM has resulted in a default strategy. When our strategy is to "split the difference" between our offer and our counterpart's offer it naturally follows that we would establish a relatively extreme position. Since we know we will not get what we ask for, we ask for a lot more than we really think is reasonable. Unless our counterpart is ignorant, the natural response to our extreme position is to state an equally extreme position in the opposite direction.

Now what? We expend tremendous amounts of energy defending our clearly extreme position. Until when? Until a mutually perceived deadline. Then what? Some form of SIDTM behavior with predictable distasteful results. The buyer returns to his or her office and grouses, "I could have bought for less if I'd held out a little longer." The seller returns to his or her office and complains, "I could have sold for more if I'd held out a little longer." What an awful strategy! We establish extreme positions; we defend these silly positions until some perceived deadline. Then we split the difference in some fashion with predictable dissatisfaction. There must be a better way!

### *Reject the Strategy; Retain the Tactic*

The source of our solution is to understand the difference between the kinds of issues presented in any particular negotiation scenario. Principle issues and positional issues are the two most common. SIDTM is most useful in positional negotiation. However, principle negotiation should logically come first.

Fisher and Ury in their wonderful book *Getting to Yes* provide a concise explanation of the difference between principle and positional issues. The book is a tremendous addition to your negotiation library. In short, principle issues reflect the values, objections, decisions, and interests we feel support our contemplated transactions. Positional issues represent the actual amount, place, time, or concessionary equilibrium we finally reach.

Sister is at home doing her homework at the kitchen table. Brother comes home and turns on his Offspring CD at the 150-decibel level.

Her position: "Turn that off! I can't do my homework with all that noise."

His position: "I live here too and I want to listen to my music!"

This is a common set of stand-off positions with no real apparent compromise.

Brother and sister could agree to specific times for homework and music listening. Mom and dad could eject one or both of them from the house. However, neither of these solutions offers long-term satisfaction.

They could split it down the middle and turn the music down halfway. However, this situation is only a partial resolution of their differences. The SIDTM solution builds on the seeds of mistrust.

If brother leaves the living room sister goes in and turns the music down. When he comes back he notices the reduced volume level and turns the music back up, not to the previous level but to an even higher level. She wants silence. He wants to listen to really loud music. How can they both get what they want? Headphones! Headphones allow both parties to have all of what they are looking for in this everyday example of compromise.

If we can become clear as to what we really want in a transaction and why we want it, and if we can become clear as to what our counterpart wants, and why, then a "headphones" type solution is highly probable.

## Application of the New Strategy

In sales and marketing this new principle-driven strategy is seen in the consultative selling approach. We learn what our customers want rather than simply selling them what we have. When our customers complain, we make in-depth inquiry into the sources of dissatisfaction rather than simply waving a policy manual at them.

When we seek to negotiate behavior in the workplace we honestly attempt to understand the reasons behind our employees conduct rather than make threats about their continued employment. A "headphones" type solution is potentially possible in almost every negotiation scenario. But we need to spend time and effort working toward that solution. If not, we fall back into the old patterns.

### SIDTM is a great tactic, but it's a lousy strategy.

By the way, I bought the T-Bird for $800 and sold it two years later for $1,200. I thought I was a genius! I wish I still owned that car today.

• • •

# CHAPTER EIGHT

# How to Make the Other Side Play Fair

WHEN YOU TALK ABOUT NEGOTIATING ON A MATURE LEVEL OR THE win-win style of negotiating that has come into fashion in the last couple of decades, people tend to imagine a bunch of nice guys sitting around making concessions to each other. The following scenario depicts an accurate reflection of that misperception.

> *Sandra*: "Mr. Sampson, you've told me that your primary objective for your department is to increase production without sacrificing quality. I believe our product could help you meet that goal. Tell me, what do you think?"

*Mr. Sampson*: "From what you've shown me, your product seems to have potential. But I'm only interested if we can install your product on a trial basis, just to make sure it will suit our needs."

*Sandra*: "That's not a problem. I think a fair trial period would be six months. That way, your people will have ample opportunity to familiarize themselves with the procedure for using our product. You could get an accurate picture of what the product can do for you."

*Mr. Sampson*: "That sounds fair."

*Sandra*: "The cost of installing the Beta XZ200 for your use for six months will be $10,000."

*Mr. Sampson*: "That's quite a bit more than I was planning to invest in a trial run."

*Sandra*: "I can understand your position. How about $7,500?"

*Mr. Sampson*: "OK. Can we get it up and running by January 1st?"

*Sandra*: "I have to say no. We have a pretty tight production schedule and that's only two weeks away. Toward the end of January would be a more realistic delivery and installation date."

*Mr. Sampson*: "I can live with that. But I do have to insist on deferred payment. I want to make sure the system works before we pay any money on this project."

*Sandra*: "Well, normally we expect a 50 percent down payment before we install equipment on site. But if you don't want to do that, we can defer your payment until the first of February."

*Mr. Sampson*: "That's what I wanted to hear."

This exchange is not a realistic example of mature, ethical negotiations. It's not giving in on every demand. It's not satisfying someone else's needs at the expense of your own. It's not making concessions without asking for anything in return.

Mature negotiation isn't the equivalent of handing over all your marbles. I am a firm believer in getting what you want out of negotiations. Look again at Sandra and Mr. Sampson's meeting, only this time they'll be focusing on finding mutually beneficial solutions, not just giving in to each other's demands.

*Sandra*: "Mr. Sampson, we've examined the operation of your department and determined that your primary objective is to increase production without sacrificing quality. We've also established that Super Technology's Beta XZ200 can enable you to reach that goal by standardizing production and maximizing the output of your current staff and equipment."

*Mr. Sampson*: "From what you have shown me, the XZ200 appears to meet our needs. But how can we be sure? I'd like to use the equipment on a trial basis, just to make sure it will suit our needs."

*Sandra*: "Your request isn't unreasonable. The Beta XZ200 is state-of-the-art, and its installation requires a significant investment of capital. As a matter of fact, we've worked out similar arrangements with other clients, who, without exception, purchased the equipment because of the remarkable results it produced for them. We can install the Beta XZ200 for your use for six months for $10,000. In that length of time, you and your staff will have ample opportunity to familiarize yourselves with proper operating procedures for using the equipment for maximum performance."

*Mr. Sampson:* "That's a pretty steep price for a trial run, don't you think? I don't know if my company is willing to let go of that much capital just to test equipment."

*Sandra:* "Mr. Sampson, I know $10,000 sounds like a lot, but let me explain our position. The Beta XZ200 is a sophisticated piece of equipment. Only highly-skilled technicians can install it, and it usually takes at least a day. Even shipping the equipment to your facility requires special handling. We also have support personnel who will have to work with your staff to educate them on the XZ200's functions and operation. Plus, you have access to our 24-hour operation hotline for the duration of the trial period. Because of the complexity of this state-of-the-art equipment, Super Technologies can't afford to offer businesses this special arrangement without charging $10,000."

*Mr. Sampson:* "That makes sense, but you have to understand, we have only a certain amount of money budgeted for capital outlay. If I spend $10,000 on a trial run, I'm cutting into my funds for the purchase of any equipment."

*Sandra:* "That's not a problem. When you decide to buy the Beta, the $10,000 installation fee goes toward the total purchase price. After all, the system will have already been installed. Your company will be on our records and accounts. Much of the support work will have been completed. And that's what the $10,000 covers."

Do you get the idea now? Sandra and Mr. Sampson were working together to arrive at a fair and feasible arrangement for the purchase of some equipment. Neither was out to see what they could get for nothing, or how much they could get away with. They both want Mr. Sampson's organization to buy the Beta XZ200, if it fills the company's needs. So, their negotiations focused on arriving at an equitable, mutually beneficial agreement.

Now some people, the thrill seekers, also complain that the win-win negotiators of the world are draining the excitement out of negotiation.

They ask: "What about the exhilaration of victory that pumps through your system when you've pulled off a negotiating coup? What about watching out for number one? What about the American tradition of winning?"

I say, "What about the thrill of aligning people's needs, overcoming their fears, and looking for the less-than-obvious solutions? What about the satisfaction of knowing you were able to help others in addition to helping yourself? What about the long-term benefits of building productive relationships as well as profitable agreements?"

Negotiating on a mature level doesn't mean you give up everything at the bargaining table. It doesn't mean that you don't try to win. Every time I meet with someone to negotiate, my primary objective is to get the best deal possible. I enjoy winning, and if I may say so myself, I have a long list of victories. But that doesn't mean I've left a trail of losers in my wake. Putting other people out of business, figuratively speaking, isn't a requisite part of winning as a negotiator. To win on a consistent basis, as a matter of fact, depends on negotiating so that everyone involved profits from the experience. That approach to negotiating is much more challenging—not to mention more rewarding—than leaving your negotiating opponents battered and bleeding as you swagger off with the spoils of your conflict. Negotiating on a mature, adult-to-adult level doesn't take the thrill out of haggling over terms and agreements. Trying to achieve this level of relating and negotiating has its own special brand of excitement and satisfaction.

## • Negotiating Ethically Is Not for Sissies

Negotiating isn't easy, no matter what your style. Negotiating to get what you want takes brains and backbone, regardless of whether you're gunning for your negotiating counterparts, or focusing on designing equitable solutions. You have to think through what you want and the most effective way to get it. And you have to have the moxie to follow through with your plans. Sometimes simply asking for something takes nerve. After all, some of us were taught as children not to ask for anything; instead, we were to wait until it was offered. That courtesy may have won you points with your second-grade teacher, but it'll kill you in the real world. We usually have to go after what we want. And to get what we want, we have to be shrewd negotiators, even when we try to maintain high ethical standards.

As a matter of fact, negotiating on a mature, adult-to-adult basis is even more demanding than slipping around and trying to manipulate or trick the people with whom you're negotiating.

First of all, being open and honest takes guts. It takes nerve to say to the people you're negotiating with, "I want to play fair. How about you?" or "This is what I want. How about you, and how can we both get what we want?" You're challenging them to meet you on your level, and you're asking them to focus on more than their individual needs. You can get some strange reactions because people aren't used to an open approach to negotiating. Some people don't want to negotiate that way, which brings me to a second reason ethical negotiations can be so challenging. Making sure that you don't get manipulated by someone who is not as honest takes savvy.

## • How to Avoid Being Manipulated

A difference in standards can cause serious problems when negotiating. Just because you follow all the principles I outline throughout *Smart Negotiating*, that doesn't guarantee that everyone you negotiate with will be as mature and fair-minded as you are. (I know that once you've learned all my negotiating secrets, you're going to be mature and fair-minded, right?) You have to be prepared to encounter less-than-honest bargainers, people who have their eye on the prize and have no qualms about running over you to get it.

These people have no interest in forging mutually beneficial agreements. They are only interested in what's good for them, and they don't mind abusing others to get it. They are the hardballers. They want to play rough. They don't care if there's such a thing as principled negotiating. They think they can get more by bullying the people they negotiate with. They believe they're stronger than their opponents and think they can walk away with the spoils if they go for the jugular vein.

Don't misunderstand me. Not every person you meet at the negotiating table is going to be an unscrupulous rogue. Some people don't share your high standards for negotiating because they don't know any better. Before reading this book, what were your attitudes toward negotiating? Did you see it as a "me-against-my-opponent" proposition? Did you feel like the only way you could win was for someone else to lose? Some people don't realize there's a better, easier way to negotiate.

I have a system for negotiating that can handle any of the problems that inevitably crop up when I'm with people from either group.

## • Defense Tactic 1: Maintain Your Standards
If a person approaches negotiations aggressively out of ignorance, I can eventually win him or her over to my style. Most people don't want to be enemies. They just don't want to get ripped off. If you can demonstrate to them that you're interested in a fair deal, they will usually drop the aggressive routine and start to work with you.

I use this same tactic with shady negotiators. I make it a policy to never compromise my standards just because someone else seems to have no scruples. I once read a great saying: "When you fight with a pig, you both get dirty, but the pig likes it." In other words, even if you win, you've lost. Don't let people with low or no standards drag you down to their level. The bottom line is this: If you want to fight, don't let anybody talk you into negotiating; but if you want to negotiate, don't let anybody goad you into fighting.

### • *Defense Tactic 2: Protect Yourself by Not Fighting Back Directly*

When you meet with the people who don't want to play fair, you can protect yourself, and you don't have to resort to trickery or manipulation to do it.

If you think about it, most sharks are propelled by three basic drives—greed, self-centeredness, and an exaggerated ego. And any of those three drives makes them extremely vulnerable to a smart negotiator.

Roger Fisher and William Ury call this approach "negotiation jujitsu" in their book *Getting to Yes*. Jujitsu is a form of martial arts that focuses on deflecting attacks rather than engaging the enemy. If someone is running toward you aggressively, you don't stand your ground and hit back when they run into you. You step to the side and let them run past. Very simply, you don't resist the other party. When they insist on their position, you don't counterattack with your own position. Instead you say something like, "Why do feel that's the only option?" Or you can ask, "How do you think that will affect me?" Or here's a good one, "Why would I want to do that?" Don't be aggressive or belligerent. Just ask for an honest explanation of why their offer is the best solution for both parties. Make them think about and talk about their position.

When those you're negotiating with attack your position or your ideas, ask for more specific input. Ask them to explain exactly what they don't like about your ideas. Invite criticism. That'll blow their minds. When you take this approach, you are forcing the other side to work with you to forge an agreement that will benefit you and them. And they may not even realize that is what you are doing.

Fighting with others head-to-head is always difficult and usually less productive than for two parties to work together to reach an acceptable agreement. For example, a friend told me about an episode in which a savvy shipping dock foreman at a seafood distribution center used a cool head to defuse an explosive truck driver. The truck driver came bouncing up on the dock, demanding that his truck be unloaded within one hour. The foreman explained that about a half dozen trucks were in line ahead of him, and that it's first come, first served. He told the truck driver all the staff was working as hard as they could and they would get to him as soon as possible. The driver bellowed, "I don't give a damn how many trucks you've got. I've got to be on the road in one hour and that's all there is to it."

The foreman calmly replied, "I know you're under pressure to stay on the road and I'd like to help you, but we have to be fair. You'll just have to wait your turn." The truck driver was about to burst. He shouted, "I've got 15 tons of frozen Maine lobsters on that truck, and if I'm not on that loading dock in ten minutes, I'm going to start unloading them into your parking lot. Do you understand what I'm saying?"

Amazingly, the foreman remained cool. He said, "That should have some interesting results."

The truck driver growled, "What do you mean by that?"

"Well, this is a pretty tough neighborhood," the foreman said. "I'd be willing to bet money that the people around here would run off with them about as fast as you could unload them. They don't get too much lobster on this side of town."

Suddenly, the truck driver remembered the expensive cargo was his responsibility until he had a signed receipt for it. His hostility quickly faded. "How long do you reckon I'll have to wait?" he asked meekly.

Apathy can be a powerful form of negotiating jujitsu when you find yourself dealing with a jackass, as this guy certainly was. Don't forget the old axiom that the person who cares the most stands to gain the least out of any negotiation. Certainly, the dock foreman had the upper hand in that situation and he was smart enough to recognize it. But let me make a point here: we're almost always in a better negotiating position than we think we are.

The business owner who flies off the handle and threatens to fire everybody in the place if certain unreasonable demands aren't met is a good example of a person who seems to hold all the cards, but actually is in a relatively weak position. What if everybody walks out? Who's going to process orders? Who's going to handle the irate customers? Who's going to lose the most money? You guessed it, the head honcho.

Whenever you're negotiating, remember that you're a human being and you have the right to be treated like one. And I'll let you in on a little secret: Tough cookies are almost always bluffing, and they do it so often because nobody dares to call their bluff. If you just calmly refuse to play by their rules, more often than not they'll back down.

### • Defense Tactic 3: Call in a Third-Party Arbitrator

Rarely in my experience as a lawyer and a businessman have I ever had to call in a third-party arbitrator because the people I was negotiating with insisted on using less-than-honorable techniques. It almost never reaches this point. But probably most of us have been involved in situations where we needed someone who was completely impartial and had no links to anyone in the negotiations to help guide the negotiating process.

The benefit of bringing in a third party is that they can shift the negotiations from positional bargaining to bargaining based on interests. A third party can look at all sides objectively and weave together a plan that considers everyone's interests. In the next chapter, I talk about the value of third parties to get through impasses, but they work just as effectively as a means to cut through other people's attempts to manipulate you. Ideally, it's better if the primary parties involved in negotiations can work out an agreement between themselves. But it's good to know there is an option if you can't make any progress.

### • Defense Tactic 4: Bailout

When all else fails and you can't persuade the other party or parties to negotiate honestly and openly, and a mediator doesn't work, abandon the negotiations, at least for a while. Maybe a deal just wasn't meant to be. Sometimes you get a gut feeling telling you to get out of a certain negotiating situation. Go with it. Remember, you will be negotiating from a much stronger position if you are willing to walk away from the bargaining table. Maybe both parties need more time to think about what they want and what they are willing to give for it.

Certainly, walking out is a drastic, last-resort tactic, but sometimes it's the only way to get people to play fair. The way you walk out, however, can have a tremendous impact on the results your action produces. If you say, "I need some time to think this over," or "I have to consult with somebody," you're implying that you'll consider your opponent's position. This tactic is great if you're dealing with people who're negotiating in good faith. It can help you buy a little time to gather more information and plan new strategies.

If you're dealing with a shark, however, saying, "I need some time," is tantamount to raising a white flag. You're sending the message, "I recognize that my only option is to go along or not to go along with your proposal." If you return to the negotiating table, your position is extremely weak.

On the other hand, if you withdraw by saying, "Let me know if you decide to accept my offer," that's like saying, "This is my position, take it or leave it." That statement effectively ends the negotiation, unless your opponent has no choice but to go along.

Another option would be to say something like, "Obviously, we're not getting anywhere. Why don't we both just think about it for a while? If either of us comes up with a new idea we might both be able to live with, we can get back together." That way, either party could call a meeting without losing face, and equally important, you're leaving your options open.

## • Tolerance and Integrity

Negotiating is a complex process, even under the best of circumstances. Every person involved in a negotiation brings to the event a different background, culture, perceptions, values, and standards. Breaking through these differences can seem impossible, yet it is crucial to creating a mutually beneficial agreement. Maintain your standards throughout negotiations.

If you can't win cooperation, chances are you will gain nothing from the negotiations. When you encounter people who aren't negotiating ethically, try to bring them up to your level. If the other party doesn't respond to your attempts to do so, be willing to walk away. You won't have lost anything.

## *One Last Thought . . .*

### *An Oral Contract Isn't Worth the Paper It's Written On*

Friends and colleagues ask me all the time, "John, what kinds of things should I include in my written contract for a car? For a new home purchase? In a business transaction?" I have always found it helpful to use a checklist as a reminder of potential issues to consider.

Here are some of the things on my checklist that may be useful to you. The entire checklist can be found in *How to Build a More Lucrative Law Practice* by Noel Stevenson.

*Definitions*: Define any terms used in the contract that are open to interpretation, but remember that definitions are dangerous.

*Parties*: Names and addresses of parties. Avoid using "party of the first part," "party of the second part." Instead, identify parties by "Smith" and "Jones," "buyer" and "seller," "Lessor" and "Lessee," or "Exclusive Agent."

*Legal status*: Ascertain the marital or legal status of the parties.

*Date of execution*: The date of the contract. It is advisable to avoid the use of an "as of" date, as it indicates that the contract was not signed on that date.

*Effective date*: The effective date of the contract.

*Arbitration*: Provision for arbitration disputes.

*Age and competence*: Are the parties competent to contract? It isn't advisable to rely on appearances, sometimes an 18-year-old looks and acts over 21. As for mental competency, usually all one can do is observe and hope for the best.

*Jurisdiction*: Consider including a recital of the law of what jurisdiction should apply to the contract.

*Time is of the essence*: Is it advisable to provide a timeline in the contract?

*Performance duties*: Include in specific terms what performance each of the parties is liable for and the time each obligation is to be performed.

*Future changes to the law*: Make provisions for any future change of the law or administrative regulations that would affect the parties.

*Performance/reason for delays in*: Make provisions for strikes, acts of war, acts of God, or any other catastrophes that prevent or delay performances of one of the parties.

*Consideration*: What is the consideration of the contract?

*Modification*: Provide that any modification of contract must be in writing.

*Payment of money*: State the time and place of payment of any money.

*Damages/default*: Provide for damages, if any should be paid, in case of the default of a party.

*Cancellation/provision for*: If any party to the contract has a right to cancel the contract, include provision for such cancellation.

*Paragraph headings*: Consider including paragraph headings such as "Insurance," "Notices," and "Covenant Not to Compete." If these paragraph headings are included, provide in the contract that these subject headings are for the sake of convenience and are not a part of the contract.

### Conclusion

Good luck with your agreements. Remember the most important thing in writing an agreement is that it should be designed to provide for real or potential ambiguities and difficulties, not for litigation. Unless your contract concerns high six-figure agreements, you should stay away from lawyers and litigation—it's too expensive, trust me! Remember, every one of these issues is negotiable. Use this checklist and you will be able to Negotiate like the Pros.

· · ·

# CHAPTER NINE

# Breaking
# Impasses

B Y FOLLOWING MY STRATEGY FOR NEGOTIATING, YOU WILL encounter fewer impasses. When all the parties involved in negotiations are sincerely interested in producing an agreement that will meet everyone's needs, they are less likely to get hung up on insignificant issues, and they are willing to make compromises. That's one of the most valuable aspects of the Dolan Strategy for negotiating like the pros. Stalls and snags are almost always easier to prevent than they are to overcome.

That explains my focus on effective communication throughout this book. If people can reach a mature level of understanding early in negotiations and maintain that ability to relate to one another throughout the process, they can avoid the impasses that threaten to block productive solutions. And believe me, no matter how difficult it may seem at the time, it's almost always easier to keep negotiations moving than to get them started again.

To give you an idea of the cost of inadequate communication, I can honestly say that most of the divorce cases my legal firm has handled over the years never would have reached the inside of a courtroom if the people involved had been able to communicate effectively with each other. The inability to communicate, however, undermines a couple's relationship and makes it impossible for them to resolve differences. A similar series of breakdowns can happen at a negotiating table where people are not communicating.

Even under the best of circumstances, however, the decision-making process in negotiations can hit a stone wall. So, the Dolan Strategy for more effective negotiation wouldn't be complete without a survival kit on breaking through impasses at the bargaining table.

## • Pinpointing the Problem

We've all been there. The people we're negotiating with are being cooperative. We're all able to talk openly about our positions, our interests, and our concerns. We have the issues spelled out, and negotiations seem to be headed on a course for success. Then, without warning, discussions hit a snag, and all progress is halted.

This experience can be extremely frustrating, because, for some reason—I'll call it Dolan's Law—you don't usually hit snags until after you've invested endless hours and tremendous effort in reaching an agreement. And because you've come so far, pinpointing one particular problem can be a complicated task. You may have to peel back several layers of misunderstandings or misperceptions before you can get negotiations back on track. Stalled negotiations can be blamed on any number of elements.

### • Reason 1: A Lack of Understanding Between Negotiating Parties

I touched on this problem in the opening of this chapter. If people can't understand each other, they will have a hard time reaching a mutually satisfying agreement. Of course, most of us tend to feel that it's the other party who doesn't understand us, not vice versa. Part of the problem is semantics. Somehow, we seem to think that understanding and agreeing are the same thing. In other words, if I understand what you say, that means I agree with what you say.

Think about it for a minute. There is no single word or idiomatic expression in the English language that conveys all the shades of meaning involved in saying, "I understand what you have said, and I neither agree nor disagree." Even if you say those words, it comes across like, "Oh, I understand what you're saying, but I don't really care." So what do we do? We try to counter everything the other people say, because we don't want them to think we agree with it. The net result is that we convey the feeling that we don't understand where they're coming from and maybe we don't even want to understand.

The only hope we have for breaking through all that junk is to go out of our way to let people know that we're trying to understand them and their needs. If people believe you understand and care, you can work out almost any difficulties in defining terms. If, however, they think you don't understand or care, you can talk forever and never reach an agreement.

One good technique for conveying understanding is to feed back what the person has just said to us. You might say, "So, what you're really saying is . . ." Then you summarize what the person has just said. That lets him or her know that you've really heard it.

### • Reason 2: Emotions

People often get emotionally involved in their dealings with others. They get angry or their feelings get hurt, yet they don't want to abandon negotiations. I know it's hard not to get emotionally involved when you're haggling over critical issues. I've been guilty of that myself.

But, boy, can it cost you. I knew a woman who wouldn't agree to sell her house to a couple because their first offer was too low. "Insultingly low" is how she described it. We're talking about a woman who took great pride in keeping her home beautiful. She loved her house, and she was moving only because her husband was transferred.

The people who were making an offer on the house didn't realize the judgments they made about the house were, in essence, judgments of her. So, when their first offer was turned down, they made a second offer, which would have been satisfactory from any other prospect. But the seller wouldn't budge. She insisted on getting the list price for the house. She didn't want people who couldn't appreciate the beauty of her home to have it. And besides that, she just flat out didn't like the prospective buyers. Fortunately, it was a sellers' market and somebody else bought the house relatively quickly. But I don't think that would have made one bit of difference to this woman. She would have sat there for eternity rather than sell the house to that first couple.

I think it's important to say, yes, you have a right to your feelings. But you have to make sure that exercising that right is not going to cost you more than it's worth. The important thing to remember is that getting emotional over an issue you're negotiating, or the way someone is acting, is not a good idea. To let wounded pride or hurt feelings be the only barrier to a good deal isn't smart.

If the woman had not been so sensitive about her house, and had accepted the buyer's second offer, she probably could have taken a lot of the hassle out of moving. Instead, selling the house became one more problem for her and her husband to deal with. Think about how unhappy the real estate agent must have been. Her refusal to sell could have caused him serious problems.

When you sense that your emotions or your ego are getting in the way of negotiation, you have to ask yourself, "Is it really worth it?" Basically, it all goes back to being a mature negotiator. Are you going to let your temper, or your thin skin, cost you a good deal? The real pros don't. They focus on the benefits of the deal, instead of dwelling on negative feelings. The only time I can imagine letting anger force you away from the table is when you sense you are being cheated, and that brings me to the third reason negotiations collapse.

## • *Reason 3: Dishonesty at the Negotiating Table*

When I talk about dishonesty in negotiations, I'm talking about lying or promising things you know you can't deliver. I'm not referring to some of the questionable tactics we covered earlier. Those maneuvers might not be exactly ethical, but most people aren't surprised to see them in negotiations. Experienced negotiators treat them as part of the game.

Take a look at an example of what I mean by dishonesty. I hate to use this cliché, but let's say you're negotiating with a car dealer. He assures you that his mechanics have checked out the vehicle and it's in perfect running condition. So yes, he is asking top dollar for it. Then, you take the car for a test drive—straight to your mechanic, who tells you that the transmission is about to fall out and needs to be replaced immediately. He doesn't think you're even going to make it back to the car lot. Now that car dealer is out of luck. Not only are you not going to buy the lemon he's trying to pawn off on you, you'll never put your foot on his lot again. And you'll warn all your friends to steer clear of him. That's dishonest negotiation, and that's the kind of price people can pay for it.

## • Getting Negotiations Going Again

Hitting a glitch doesn't necessarily spell disaster for negotiations. Usually, once you discover the cause for the delay, you can work through the difference and resume progress. The best thing to do when you hit a snag is to try to diagnose the problem. Determine why you are snagged. Start by asking yourself and everyone else involved in the negotiations these questions:

- Do we understand the issues being negotiated?
- Have both parties been able to describe their position, interests, and desires thoroughly?
- Do both parties understand each other's interests and positions?
- Just exactly what does everyone want?

Just back up and make sure everyone understands what's being negotiated and what everyone wants. Getting back to the issues can often reveal the point of contention that's blocking agreement.

Knowing what's at stake, however, and clarifying what everyone wants and what the issues are, doesn't guarantee people can smoothly work through their differences. Solutions are proposed, but one side or the other shoots them down. Sometimes, this pattern can go on forever. Let me share with you several tactics for overcoming such impasses.

### • *Tactic 1: Return to a Prior Agreement*

Returning to a prior agreement causes everyone to focus on the positive breakthroughs you've made up to the point at which you hit the snag. This tactic usually gives the parties hope that you can resolve the deadlock.

As you review any prior agreements, you can say, "Look, we've come so far. We've worked through this problem, which we thought was insurmountable. And we've settled all these points. Surely, we can come up with some solution on this issue. What do you think?" Sometimes this glance backward is just enough to nudge people into working out compromises and focusing on the big picture, instead of getting hung up on a single point.

### • *Tactic 2: Take a Hypothetical Approach to a Suggested Option That Is Causing the Stalemate*

Present the option in question, and say, "Imagine if we did it this way. Let's look at all the possible consequences." Approaching a problem from this angle enables you to zero in on the individual points that are causing the delay.

This tactic forces you to examine closely all the elements involved in pursuing the option, and that process usually reveals exactly what people don't like about it. By doing this, you might discover that a small adjustment would make the option acceptable. This approach can prevent you from abandoning the suggestion completely and returning to the drawing board.

### • Tactic 3: Point Out the Negative Consequences if the Other Person Won't Make a Decision or Agree to a Concession

This tactic is one of the strongest you can use to break an impasse. I pull this one out when I think nothing less than a stick of dynamite is going to dislodge the objections blocking progress in negotiations. Say you were in a car accident, your car was totaled, and you're negotiating with the insurance company for a settlement. The insurance company is giving you the runaround and is trying to get you to accept an amount that is far below what you have calculated the car to be worth. If discussions don't seem to be getting anywhere, you can say something like, "If we can't settle this to my satisfaction today, I'll be forced to contact my lawyer." Quite often, that will at least get their attention.

Speaking of negotiating with a company, let me slip in a piece of advice here. Always locate one person within a company with whom to negotiate. Don't let the individuals within an organization pass you around from person to person or from department to department. That's a ploy to wear you down. Don't fall for it. Lyndon Johnson once said, "If the second person you talk with when you make a call can't answer your question, you're dealing with a bureaucracy." Find one representative who will handle all your calls and who will be the negotiating face for the company. This way, you're negotiating with an individual, not an intangible "they" who don't have to take responsibility or make decisions.

### • Tactic 4: Play on Your Counterpart's Emotions

I know I just finished telling you to check your emotions at the door when you walk into a room to negotiate. But that doesn't mean the people you're negotiating with have done the same thing. Sometimes all you have to do to get action is trigger their emotions.

For example, you might be working with a client, trying to make a big sale. You and this individual have been hammering out details for days. You've both invested a lot of time and energy in your negotiations and you're close to a deal, but you just can't quite get together. You can say, "Is this issue going to ruin our negotiations? Man, this is really making me feel bad. I hate that we can't seem to move forward on this."

This statement, followed by silence, can have a tremendous impact on the right person's resolve. When I say "right" person, I mean someone who is susceptible to a play on emotions. Some people are completely oblivious to the maneuver, and others will take it as a sign of weakness on your part. So, think carefully before you use it, but you'll be surprised at how often it will work.

Some people just can't stand for others around them or involved with them to feel bad. They will do what it takes to make everyone happy. I'm not suggesting that you take advantage of people who seem to fit this description. But you can use their tendencies to keep negotiations moving.

### • Tactic 5: Call a Time Out

An effective way to get action when things have bogged down at the negotiating table is to say something like, "Well, we don't seem to be making any progress, so why don't we just take some time to think about what we've accomplished so far and to consider whether we want to continue."

This approach serves two purposes:

1. It gives people a chance to cool off and to look at the situation more objectively. Maybe in the interim, someone will come up with a workable agreement.

2. It's an inoffensive yet effective way to signal the other party that you're unhappy with the terms being offered.

This approach is a final cutoff, like a "take-it-or-leave-it-statement" would be, but it does serve the purpose of letting the other party know that you're not willing to haggle over details forever.

### • *Tactic 6: Defer Issues to an Objective Third Party*

Sometimes you need to call in a neutral or objective third party, someone who has no interest in either side coming out ahead of the other. I believe this action is a last resort. If none of the other tactics dislodges a snag, you can always try to bring in an objective third party who can help everyone see issues more clearly and from each other's perspective. I'm talking about arbitration.

An arbitrator can look at the issues and positions without bias and propose a solution that he or she believes is best for everyone involved. If all parties can agree on taking this route, an arbitrator can sometimes solve even the toughest of stalemates.

As a very last resort, both parties can agree to submit to binding arbitration. That's where you let someone else decide, and both parties agree in advance that they will accept whatever terms are dictated. Arbitration removes control from your hands. Whether you choose this route depends on how badly you need to negotiate an agreement and what your strengths are. If you must defer negotiations to a third party, be sure that you are in a position to live with an objective decision.

## • Understanding the Impact of Personal Negotiating Style

I've touched on the idea of using certain approaches when working with different personality styles throughout this book, but I think you'll find it helpful to have a better understanding of how people's individual styles can affect negotiations. When it comes to breaking impasses, all the approaches I've talked about have to be adjusted to match the negotiating styles of the people you face on the other side of the bargaining table.

Over the years, I've found that there are basically four styles of negotiators:

1. Balkers
2. Talkers
3. Analyzers
4. Deciders

The balkers keep stalling on making any decisions. They balk at everything you say or do. Their favorite expression seems to be, "Well, I don't know . . ." These people can drive you bananas, and they can keep negotiations bogged down forever.

Next are the talkers, who want to talk any issue that comes up to death. Ask a question or make a proposal and that sets them off on a tangent. They often say, "You know, that reminds me of the time when . . . blah, blah, blah!" Talkers can eat up endless hours and make progress almost impossible.

The third negotiating style is the analyzers. These people want to look at every issue from every conceivable direction—and some directions that are inconceivable. They're a little like the balkers, except that their problem is not indecision, but rather wanting to make sure they cover every minute detail. Their favorite expression is, "Now, let's look at that a little more closely." They can wear everybody out going over the same ground again and again.

Finally, you have the deciders. These people don't care about the details, they don't see a need to talk things to death, and they hate indecisive people. They just want to get to the bottom line and make a decision. You'll most often hear them say, "Let's get this show on the road!" When you get two or more of these styles together, which happens more often than not, it's like trying to mix oil and water. No matter how much you stir, the two never combine. Negotiations can bog down, and getting them moving again is almost impossible. You can, however, meet with all these styles and still build an agreement acceptable to everyone.

Expert negotiators have learned how to be peacemakers. That's not always a comfortable role to play when you're trying to look out for your own skin at the same time. Besides, sometimes, in the heat of negotiations, people can get pretty hard on peacemakers. Because the peacemaker is trying to get everyone's perceptions aligned and trying to help people understand one another, others involved in the negotiations will often unload their frustrations on that person who seems to be in the middle of things.

Being a peacemaker is worth the pressure, however, if there is any chance of reaching a strong, productive, and mutually beneficial agreement. As peacemaker, try to help everyone see each other's position. One way to do it is to focus on the process itself, instead of on the individuals involved.

For instance, if you sense that negotiations are beginning to slow down, you can say something like, "I sense that there are some strong feelings on all sides here. Maybe it would be a good idea to set up a format in which everybody can be heard and nobody feels pressured." Then, suggest a procedure.

Obviously, the type of procedure you choose depends a great deal on the complexity of the issues and the circumstances under which you're negotiating. For instance, if you're dealing with major issues and a lot of people are involved, follow some formal procedure, like the Senate rules or Robert's Rules of Order. At least set up an orderly way to control the introduction of ideas and proposals. You might even consider setting some time limits on debating each issue. This tactic will keep everybody under control, even the talkers.

Sometimes it helps to designate a committee to create a basic working document and bring it back to the group for consideration. It's almost always easier to work from and amend something than to try to start from scratch.

Keep in mind that you can't make much progress wandering around lost in a fog. It's second nature in negotiations for people to throw out all their smoke screens, making the situation more and more murky. So make it a practice to constantly cut through the smoke screens and make sure you are always talking about substantive issues—no matter who you're dealing with or what their personality styles are.

## • Break Impasses without Giving In

If you review the tactics covered in this chapter, you'll notice they all have at least one trait in common. They are designed to enable you to unlock stalemates without giving in. I've seen more than a few cases where people have given away the store because they were desperate to close negotiations. When someone raised an objection to a proposal or option, the other party would make concessions just to salvage the negotiations. This is so common, in fact, that some negotiators will stage a deadlock to force the other party to give in to their demands. I don't recommend using this sleazy tactic, but be aware that some people will have no qualms about using it against you.

Certainly, it's important to clear up any dissension that is impeding progress, but that doesn't mean you have to start making concessions. Always look for ways to resume negotiations without making sacrifices. Focus on creating better understanding between the negotiating parties, and look for solutions that will meet everyone's needs.

## • Walking Away

Every once in a while you're going to hit such a major snag that you don't have any choice but to walk away. If you've tried every approach you can imagine, and you still can't work out a deal that's good for you, give up. Cut your losses and get out of there. You're probably sick of hearing me say this, but you don't have to accept a deal that's going to hurt you. You can always walk away.

## *One Last Thought . . .*

### *Warm Nuts and a Moist Towlette or How to Negotiate Your Way Down the Road*

My wife, Irene, and I dreaded a trip in coach. We had obtained two frequent flyer program tickets on American Airlines departing from Orange County heading to Dallas, Texas. While riding in Coach is not as difficult as traveling in the rowing section of a slave galley, it's close. What to do?

You can never get a First Class upgrade from a frequent flyer mileage ticket . . . or can you?

The Platinum desk repeated the policy to me over the phone. The counter personnel laughed at my request. The gate personnel rolled their eyes. My last chance was the flight attendant.

Handing my book *Negotiate like the Pros* to the flight attendant with the inscription,

> *Thank you for the complimentary First Class upgrade you are about to give my wife and me!*

I held my breath.

"Ha-ha!" she said. "Sorry, but you know I can't."

"That's OK," I replied, "it never hurts to give it one more try!"

Then, right before the aircraft pushed back, the flight attendant waved at me to come forward.

First Class to Dallas! And they said it couldn't be done! The glamour of travel wears thin for many seasoned veterans. Shortcuts, time, and money savings techniques are a big part of the road warrior's survival. Deals with air carriers, hotels, ground transportation providers, and restaurants are plentiful and fun to make.

### Air Travel

Pick one or more:

Flying is fun.

Flying is awful.

Flying is boring.

Flying is a necessary evil.

Flying is nerve wracking.

All of the above.

None of the above.

### Frequent Flyers

Frequent flyer programs can help smooth the way for the frequent traveler. American Airlines, United Airlines, Northwest, Continental, and a number of other carriers allow for bonus travel and benefits for frequent flyers. Belonging to one or more of these programs is essential to the experienced traveler. Many of the major domestic American carriers are members of World Wide Alliances. American Airlines is allied with British Airways, Qantas, Cathay Pacific, and others. United and others have similar relationships with other major carriers.

The best part of these programs is that they are all free and available to any frequent flyer. Upgrades, special seating, advanced boarding privileges, and airport club memberships are all negotiable with one of these frequent flyer programs.

### Hotels

Starwood, Hilton, Marriott, and other major hotel chains have frequent traveler programs, too. Upgrades to suites, concierge or club levels, free nights, and travel benefits can all be negotiated with the assistance of these programs. These programs are also almost universally free to the frequent traveler.

### Restaurants

Tip on the way in. You have a better chance for good service. Ask the maitre'd for his or her suggestions. In fact, ask them to order your meal. You'll get the chef's best that evening and you'll make a friend for the future. Never send your food back. If you do, they will spit in your soup!

· · ·

# CHAPTER TEN

# Negotiate with Strength—No Matter What Your Position

IMAGINE A SALESPERSON IN AN INTENSELY COMPETITIVE MARKET glutted with comparable products and equal levels of service; an entrepreneur facing a "merge-or-be-eaten-alive" proposition from a huge corporation; a job candidate competing with dozens of other talented prospects in a saturated labor market; a lone consumer challenging a giant automaker to make amends after a car it built began to disintegrate only months after cruising off the showroom floor; a lawyer plea-bargaining for a confessed felon.

These five characters share a common dilemma: they each appear to be sitting on the losing side of the negotiating table. Failure, like an executioner's ax, looms over their heads. On the surface, these people appear powerless in the face of gargantuan enemies. They seem to have few options: raise the white flag, beg for mercy, or run away. Experience has taught me that seldom are negotiation outlooks so bleak.

## • Winning Starts in Your Mind

One reason negotiations are rarely as discouraging as they seem is that, as I said earlier, the majority of people don't want to anni-hilate you simply because they have superior firepower. The people in this category will respond positively when you intro-duce negotiations on a mature level. When you can convince them that they will gain as much, if not more, by focusing on designing collectively profitable solutions rather than winning individual positions, you will relieve much of the pressure asso-ciated with negotiating from a disadvantage.

You obviously have something they want or need, or you wouldn't be negotiating. By using the Dolan Strategy, you can demonstrate for your negotiating counterparts that they don't have to beat you up to get what they want. All parties will accomplish much more when you look for ways everyone can profit from the relationship.

Second, negotiations are usually not as impossible as they seem. At least 50 percent of your negotiating strength or weak-ness is in your mind. In other words, very few situations are as hopeless as they seem when people are desperate. The biggest obstacle to overcome is usually the one in your mind.

What Tom Peters and Bob Waterman say is true—perception is reality. The perceptions of all interested parties will almost always have more to do with the outcome of a bargaining ses-sion than the realities of the situation. I've seen it proved over and over in negotiating that what you think is what you get. If you think you are beaten, you are, but if you think you are not beaten, you may not be. You at least have a fighting chance.

What I'm talking about runs deeper than bluffing, which can be a strong negotiating tool in itself. It goes back to what I said earlier about information being power. Your first line of defense when you're up against strong forces is to find out everything you can before you start to negotiate.

For example, find out if the other side realizes how much power it has. Do they know what your weaknesses are? Do you know what their weaknesses are? And do they really want to play hardball just because they're holding a bat over your head?

I've seen people settle lawsuits out of court for ludicrous amounts or terms when they had sure cases. Why? Simply because they wanted to avoid the ordeal of going through a long, drawn-out trial. Maybe they realized winning wouldn't compensate for the cost of pressing the suit. Or maybe they were afraid of being embarrassed by all the publicity of a trial. They might even be frightened that if the courtroom procedure opened too many closet doors, some of their own skeletons would come parading out. People have all kinds of reasons to back away from crushing a bargaining opponent.

Even if you are at a disadvantage and you can't persuade the people you're negotiating with to negotiate on a mature level, you are not necessarily doomed just because the other players seem to be holding all the aces. If that were the case, poker would be nothing more than a game of chance. If you were dealt good cards, you would win. If you received a bad hand, you would lose. My Las Vegas buddies tell me that's not the way it is. The distribution of the cards is only part of the formula. Knowing what to do with what you have is the real key to winning in poker. It's also the key to winning at the negotiation table.

## • Build Your Strength through Strategy

Strength doesn't come only from the goods or services you have to trade at the bargaining table. Sometimes, your ability to negotiate is your most powerful weapon.

Your opponents may have an impregnable position, and they may be after your hide, but they may be totally inept at negotiating. Let's face it—most people are not good negotiators.

A weak position doesn't mean you have to roll over and die or cave in to whatever terms the other side demands. You have several options before you start waving a white flag. Remember David and Goliath? You're not doomed to defeat just because you're negotiating from a disadvantage. You merely have to bargain more carefully. Three tactics can protect you from yourself when you're negotiating from a weakness:

### • *Tactic 1: Avoid Making the Wrong Decision Just Because You Feel the Need to Make a Decision*

You can always decide not to decide. If you don't like what's on the table, are there any laws commanding you to accept the terms? No. Not deciding might have some consequences, but they may not be as bad as the terms being offered.

Plan to avoid being forced to accept bad terms. Here's a good example: Let's say a big storm has hit your community, and three trees have fallen on your house and car. You need to have those trees removed as soon as possible. You have a gaping hole in your roof, and the next rainstorm will spell disaster unless something is done soon. Your car looks drivable, but you can't get it out, and you need it for your work.

To make things interesting, let's say your house is paid for, and you let your insurance drop about six months earlier because you didn't have the money to pay the premiums. Obviously, saving money on repairs is critical. You dread negotiating with one of the few tree-cutting services in town to have the monsters removed. You're desperate. But let's consider some measures you could take to protect yourself from making a bad decision.

First, establish a limit on the terms you're willing to accept before you get into negotiations. How much can you afford to spend? Keep in mind it's going to cost you if you don't fix that gaping hole before the next big rain. If you don't have ready cash to pay for the repairs, talk with someone at your bank and find out what kind of loan you can get. Know exactly what you can afford before you meet with the tree cutters and roofers. Also, how long can you wait to have the work done? The tree cutters and roofers in your community are probably swamped with business because the storm blew down trees all over town. Can you afford to pay more to get the work done immediately?

As I said earlier, negotiating from a disadvantage requires you to bargain more carefully. You need to do some thorough investigating before you set your bottom line. You may feel desperate, but you don't want to create bigger problems for yourself by setting a bottom line you can't live with. Find out exactly what you can afford and how long you can wait, then set your limit.

Next, explore all your options. Get creative about it. If necessity is the mother of invention, desperation is the father of creativity. Good negotiators are usually pretty creative people. The fellow whose story inspired this scenario did not want to be taken advantage of by the price gougers, so he found a firm that owned two big truck wreckers. It took some fancy negotiating, but he talked them into bringing those wreckers to his house. They used one of them to lift the tree and the other to pull it to the side. Then the man borrowed a huge tarpaulin to cover the hole in the roof and waited until the market settled down. He figured that by getting creative, and putting up with some inconvenience, he saved himself about $5,000.

You don't know your bottom line until you've examined all your options—even the outrageous ones. Just knowing you have some options empowers you. If you know in advance what you will do if the people you're negotiating with refuse to meet your bottom line, you won't be as likely to roll over and play dead. The more options you can generate, the better you can meet the first objective of negotiating when you're at a disadvantage. Don't make the situation worse by making a bad decision.

## • Tactic 2: Focus on Your Strengths

Finding strengths that compare to the awesome power of your opponents isn't always easy. Most of us have felt at times as if we were going up against a nuclear missile with a Roman candle.

It's easy to get lost in our anxieties and convince ourselves that there's no way we can beat our opponents. We convince ourselves that they're just too strong, and we don't have a leg to stand on.

In even the worst negotiating situations, however, that's almost never true. The tree-cutting example proves that. With enough planning and forethought, you can uncover strengths. And even if they're small, it's more productive to focus on them than it is to throw up your hands and say, "We're doomed." Remember, you have something the other side wants, or they wouldn't waste their time negotiating with you.

Focus on your strengths, and you will build your confidence. When you're confident, you are less likely to make unnecessary concessions, and you will make your demands more forcefully. You will have a strong presence that earns you the respect of the people you're negotiating with, which can have a significant impact on getting your way. It's like the old poker bluff. The cards in your hand aren't as important as the look on your face. So keep your mind on your strengths.

However, I'm not talking about empty bluffing. I'm talking about taking tangible action, instead of sitting around crying about how bad your situation is. Let me remind you of an incredible example that most of us can remember vividly— Lieutenant Colonel Oliver North, the fall guy in the infamous Irangate scandal.

The media was out for blood. Lifetime political careers rested on how effectively the special prosecutor and courts could make someone pay for the things that had happened. And any Washington power broker who stood up to testify for him was facing political or career suicide.

If ever a man was negotiating at a disadvantage, Ollie North was. But what a performance he put on. He and his counsel pulled out every strength they had going for them, and used it to maximum advantage. They knew that time was on their side, so they stalled in every way possible. They knew that national security was a sacred cow, so they played it to the hilt. Partisan politics worked to their advantage, so they continuously tried to divide their interrogators along party lines.

Their real coup de grace, however, was the way they used the media. Television cameras dogged North mercilessly, and he had enough savvy to know that the networks were a lot more powerful than he was. Remember what we said about not attacking strength head on, but stepping aside and letting it stumble all over itself. That's exactly what Ollie did.

What most people call invasion of privacy, he thought of as free media advertising. He gave them a show they'd never forget. His clean cut, naïve, all-American schoolboy looks and actions made him a national hero. His sincere tone and carefully chosen words melted the hearts of the masses.

Ollie-mania broke out everywhere. People all over America were showing off "Free Ollie" T-shirts and "Ollie for President" bumper stickers. By the time the hearings were over, public sentiment had turned dramatically in his favor. The polls showed that even people who were convinced he was guilty were protesting for him to be set free.

And if you don't think public sentiment affected a supposedly unbiased jury and impartial judge at his trial, you're as naïve as old Ollie appeared to be. Compared with the sentence he could have gotten, he walked away virtually a free man.

Whether Ollie North got what he deserved is beside the point here. As an attorney and negotiation consultant, I loved the performance he and his counsel put on. It was a masterpiece of taking maximum advantage of one's strengths in the face of overwhelming odds. That's exactly what I'm suggesting you do.

## • Tactic 3: Take Full Advantage of Your Counterpart's Weaknesses

The only weaknesses you should focus on are your opponent's. The people you're negotiating with are bound to have at least one or two weaknesses, so look for them. Try to find any crack in their armor before you begin negotiating, so you can work it into your plans. Some weaknesses are obvious. You can find them by researching the situation and the people involved. What you don't find in your preliminary research, you can uncover once you begin negotiating, especially by asking questions. As you know, questions can be one of your most powerful negotiating tools. If you use them well, especially when you let enough negative facts about your opponents slip out to make them wonder how much you know, questions can either lead you to undiscovered weaknesses or cause your opponents to back off on their demands.

Of course, looking for weaknesses doesn't necessarily imply digging up dirt or moral imperfections. What we're talking about are weaknesses in their bargaining positions—very practical considerations that those who seem to hold all the cards must consider before trying to pin your hide to the wall.

Here's an example based on my experience as a trial lawyer. Many of the people I defend have been charged with serious crimes and would seem to have little or no bargaining power. The evidence seems stacked against them, and very often the prosecutors are out for blood. If their cases ever go to trial, they're sunk. What can they do? How can I negotiate with the prosecutors on their behalf? Well, very often, there is a clue in the statement I just made "If their cases ever go to trial . . ."

The courts have long recognized the practicality of what's known in the legal profession as plea bargaining. That's where an accused person enters a plea of guilty to a lesser charge; the prosecution accepts the lesser plea, and the judge sentences the accused accordingly.

Now why would a prosecutor accept a plea bargain when he or she has a solid case against the person? There are a number of reasons why it makes sense. First, a district attorney's office may have so many cases backed up waiting for trial that they are forced to look for ways to dispose of some of them quickly. And there's always the problem of a person being entitled to a timely trial. If the DA's case load is such that the person can't be tried for months, or the courts are overloaded so badly a judge can't hear the case for maybe a year or more, that could raise some definite problems.

The DA must also look at the seriousness of the charge compared to other high-priority cases that have to be prosecuted. Then there's always the cost factor of a long, drawn-out trial. And how solid is the evidence, really? Is it possible that an arresting officer made a mistake that could get the charge against my client thrown out of court? The prosecution could always make a mistake in presenting its case, and juries are notoriously unpredictable. A sure plea of guilty to a lesser charge might be a safer bet than facing all the uncertainties of a trial.

As if all that were not enough to consider, what does society do with an accused felon who's waiting for months to come to trial? Do you turn him loose on bail and hope he doesn't commit another crime? Do you keep him locked up in a seriously overcrowded jail? The public doesn't understand all this, but the courts have definite limitations in budgets, staff availability, and facilities. When you add it all up, our seemingly impregnable legal system has a lot of holes in it. Sometimes, it makes very good sense to allow an accused felon to plead guilty to a lesser charge. Therefore, any trial lawyer spends a great deal of time negotiating plea-bargain arrangements for clients.

Now I don't want to get into the morality of copping pleas. That's not the issue we're concerned with. I'm talking about the fact that almost anybody you are negotiating with has weaknesses in his or her bargaining position. If you can find those weaknesses, you add strength to your own negotiating position. You see, the real issue is not necessarily the weakness in your bargaining position, but the strength of your opponent's position relative to yours. Negotiation is always a two-way street. In this world, there is no such thing as an irresistible force or an immovable object. Virtually anything is negotiable.

## • When All Else Fails

The fact is, there will be times when your back is really against the wall and your opponent is closing in. Remember, you do have options in even the darkest of negotiating situations. You may be desperate but you can choose from the following three negotiating ploys that might just save your skin:

1. Bluffing,
2. Running, and
3. Begging for mercy.

Bluffing means acting as if your position is stronger than it really is. Keep in mind what I said earlier about perceptions and realities. If you can't find a weakness in your opponent's position or strength in your position, sometimes you can create a perception of a weakness or strength.

Some classic examples can be found in the myriad of TV episodes that have been built around the old plot of making vicious crooks turn on each other. Some poor, helpless kidnap victim is begging for her life. She plants a completely baseless seed of doubt about one of her abductors in the mind of his partner in crime. Pretty soon, they're at each other's throats and she's well on her way to freedom. To me, that's a clear case of an underdog out-negotiating an opponent.

Running as a negotiating tactic simply means to lie low and make your opponent come after you. A colleague of mine who runs a small business was faced by a very large bank wanting to cancel a major contract because it had a new CEO who wanted to undo everything that had been done by the previous CEO. According to the terms of the contract, the bank had paid nearly half a million dollars more than the small firm could justify in services rendered up to that point. There were also some holes in the contract. The bank threatened to sue.

My friend's attorneys told him that in a legal battle, the bank could probably either get most of its money back—which he couldn't pay—or tie up his assets in court long enough to bankrupt him. What did my friend do? He just sat tight and said, "I'm going to make that big bank come after me." The ax never fell. An officer in the bank later told my friend that the bank's board of directors had looked long and hard at the impact of negative publicity on the public's perception of the bank. They knew the cost of consumers' seeing them as a giant bank crushing a small entrepreneur and decided it wasn't worth the risk involved in a nasty fight. They renegotiated the contract, were tickled pink with the services they received, and eventually contracted with the entrepreneur for additional services.

Making your opponents come after you can sometimes be a very effective negotiating technique. I don't suggest you try it without competent professional advice, but it's at least an option to consider.

Begging for mercy means exactly what it sounds like. It's saying to your negotiating opponent, "Look, I know you could crucify me, but I hope you won't." Let me give you two pointers to make begging for mercy as painless as possible. First, don't start begging for mercy until it's clear to everyone that you have no other options. If you've ever seen any of those old swash-buckling movies, you know what I'm talking about. The villain and the hero charge each other with their foils drawn. The sound of clashing metal erupts.

First, the hero pushes the villain against the wall, but, alas, he makes a smooth escape. Then the villain traps the hero at the top of a flight of stairs that leads to a locked door. The balance of power shifts several times, the music builds to a crescendo, and, swoosh, the hero knocks the foil from his opponent's hand and pins the evildoer to the floor. The two men face each other—the hero towering menacingly over his foe; the villain cowering on his back. After a few interminable seconds, the beaten wretch starts to beg for mercy. He waits until there's no question in any-one's mind that his life is in the hands of our champion. Then he begs for mercy.

I'm suggesting you do the same thing. Wait until it's obvious that you are at the complete mercy of your negotiating counter-parts before you start begging for compassion.

The second pointer for making the most of a bad situation is to try to offer your opponent some benefit for his or her kind-ness. Even the sniveling villain in our little scenario will usually say something like, "Spare my life, and I will take you to the princess" (who is being held captive by the rogue's accomplices, of course).

Let me reiterate: begging for mercy is a last resort. But it does work often enough to try it when all else fails.

## • A Final Word

What do these terms have in common: squeeze play, hit and run, around-the-horn, can of corn, the spitter, bender, slurve, curve, slider, shooting two, the pick-off, the hot corner, and chin music? Sports fans know these are baseball terms. They describe pitches, plays, strategies, and tactics found in America's favorite pastime.

Have you ever wondered why baseball is a favorite sport of some people and an absolute bore to others? I think people who don't like baseball just don't understand the game—the pitches, plays, strategies, and tactics. People who don't understand the game generally view baseball as a terribly slow-moving exercise punctuated by some emotional outburst between the umpires and a team's coach or manager. Maybe even a fight between the players. And then the game is over. One team wins and one team loses.

Baseball and our study of the strategy and tactics of negotiation are quite similar in several respects. It takes time and effort to understand the game. A player who understands the game has a great advantage over the player who is uninitiated. There are very basic principles that apply. The mastery of the game is in the execution of the basics.

Most people, however, understand more about baseball than they do about their everyday negotiating experiences. Because of this, some people settle for less, give up more, and generally do less well than the folks who have taken the time to learn about this vital human activity.

The fun and enjoyment a real baseball fan experiences viewing a good game is the same kind of fun and enjoyment I want you to experience every time you put together any kind of agreement. Negotiating effectively and trying to keep your bargaining on a mature level are complex endeavors. Yet, when you are successful you will reap rewards well worth the time and energy you invest in preparing your case and planning your strategy.

## One Last Thought . . .

### Negotiate with Strength
### No Matter What Your Position

Red flags. Warning signs. Flashing lights. Shrieking alarms. Any time you are negotiating and you realize you're making one of the following mistakes STOP, take a deep breath, and collect your thoughts. You may be on the slippery slope to a really poor agreement.

#### Mistake 1: Wanting Something Too Much

If you give the impression that your life depends on getting that job, car, house, or business deal, you are in trouble. Once your counterpart gets a hint of your desperation, you're dead. Remember "the person who cares least about the outcome always gets the best deal."

#### Mistake 2: Believing Your Counterpart Has All the Power

This is rarely, if ever, true. Remember, all parties want something, or they wouldn't be at the bargaining table. Ask yourself, "Why are they negotiating with me?"

#### Mistake 3: Failing to Recognize Your Own Strengths

Always try to determine your negotiating strength before you sit down at the bargaining table. The key to assessing your strengths and

·  ·  SMART NEGOTIATING   ·  ·

weaknesses is to know where you stand. Information of this kind is the true power in any negotiation.

### Mistake 4: Getting Hung Up on One Issue

This is called fixed-mind negotiating. When your counterpart uses this approach it's usually the old "red-herring." When we fall into this pattern it is usually a "pet-peeve." In any event, virtually no negotiation involves one and only one issue. If you think yours does, you are making a big mistake.

### Mistake 5: Failing to See More than One Option

Seldom do negotiations break down to only one option. There are almost always several choices of action. Creativity is the key to avoiding the "one-option" mistake.

### Mistake 6: Adopting a Win-Lose Mentality

Mutual benefit is the name of the game when the pros negotiate. If both parties are not happy, then performance becomes the problem. Anyone can shake hands on a deal. Performance only follows if benefit is derived. Otherwise, "unilateral renegotiation" is the result. Not good!

### Mistake 7: Too Much Grinding

Negotiation is a skill and an art. Understanding and using tactics is relatively simple. The real distinction between the pro and the amateur is the judgment call to end the give-and-take and proceed to performance . . . that is the art.

### Mistake 8: Short-Term Thinking

Some negotiators go for immediate payoffs, rather than seeking a long-term relationship. Long term doesn't necessarily mean over a lifetime.

It can show up later in the same negotiation session. Be careful about grinding someone down on one point. They will get you back on another issue.

### Mistake 9: Accepting Opinions, Feelings, and Statements as Facts

"Our client would never agree to a proposal such as this." "We don't feel we can pay more than $1,000 for your product." "Our budget doesn't provide for an additional installation fee." These sentences are an opinion, a feeling, and a statement. None are facts. Don't be fooled.

### Mistake 10: Accepting Firm Positions

"This is our final offer." Everyone who has any level of experience has said this, and then made another offer. Don't buy it!

### Mistake 11: Believing That Having More Authority Gives You More Negotiating Power

It is quite convenient to be able to say "I'd love to be able to work with you on these figures, Mr. Buyer, but all our prices are determined at our headquarters in Boise, Idaho. I'm afraid nothing short of a coup is going to change them."

Everyone makes mistakes. The value of becoming a student of the art of negotiation is that most of us can reduce the frequency of our mistakes and increase the frequency of optimum returns.

As an experienced negotiator, I know the strategies and tactics I've shared with you in this book produce positive results. Incorporate them into your personal style and adapt them to the individual situations you face, and you soon will be able to say "It's a Done Deal!"

• • •

# About the
# Author

S A California Criminal Trial Lawyer with decades of courtroom experience, John Patrick Dolan has handled everything from traffic tickets to death-penalty murder cases. Dolan is a recognized California State Bar Certified Specialist in Criminal Law and a true courtroom veteran. He is AV (highest) Martindale-Hubbell rated.

As an author, John Patrick Dolan has written 12 best-selling books, including his classic *Negotiate like the Pros*™. He is a recognized international authority on negotiation and conflict resolution. And just to show that he does not take himself too seriously, he is also the co-author of the wildly popular *Lawyer's Joke Book*™.

A communications veteran, John Patrick Dolan is a radio broadcaster and television legal news analyst appearing frequently on *Fox News* channel, *MSNBC*, and *Court TV*. He has also been honored by the National Speakers Association as a member of the Professional Speakers Hall of Fame.

In addition to his professional legal experience, John Patrick Dolan served as CEO of LawTalk™ MCLE, Inc., a continuing legal education company, from 1992 to 2004.

John Patrick Dolan is a native Californian. He grew up in Huntington Beach, California, "Surf City USA." He is a life-long drummer. His rock and roll band "The Wild Ones" was his passion during his younger days. His undergraduate studies at California State University, Fullerton yielded a Bachelor's degree in speech communication and political science. During his college years, John Patrick Dolan was recognized as a nationally ranked debater. His debating performance at one national event was described by Professor Laurence Tribe as a "tour de force."

John Patrick Dolan attended Western State University College of Law, from which he graduated in 1977 with a Doctor of Jurisprudence degree. During law school he served as a law clerk and sat second chair on numerous criminal cases, including several murder trials.

Additionally, he supported himself during law school as a stockbroker for Merrill Lynch. Dolan passed the California bar exam and was sworn into practice in 1978, with admission to practice in California and numerous federal jurisdictions. Additionally, he is admitted to practice before the Supreme Court of the United States of America, originally sponsored by F. Lee Bailey.

John Patrick Dolan lives in Southern California with his wife of 35 years, Irene the Queen, his daughter Andrea (A.J.), and their two Yorkshire Terriers, Jimmy and Jessie. When not involved in the practice of law, broadcasting, or professional speaking, John Patrick Dolan spends his time playing racquetball and practicing Shotokan Karate. He is a black belt!

# Glossary

**Arbitration.** The hearing and determination of a case in controversy by a person with power to decide a dispute. A third party intermediary with binding authority.

**Bluff.** To deter or frighten by pretense or a mere show of strength. To "throw a curve" at your opponent, especially when you are in a weak position.

**Concessions.** 1a) the act or an instance of conceding; b) the admitting of a point claimed in argument. Giving up an issue or a point usually in return for getting one.

**Counterpart.** One having the same function or characteristics as another. Your opponent in negotiation.

**Ethical negotiating.** Conforming to accepted professional practices of conduct in the application of standards. Keeping your standards high even when your counterpart doesn't.

**Expert negotiator.** Displaying special skill or knowledge derived from training or experience in negotiation. Someone who has practiced and mastered the skills covered in this book.

**Follow-through.** The act of fulfilling the items and details set forth in a negotiation. Doing what you promise to do, when you promise to do it, without excuses.

**Impasse.** A predicament affording no obvious escape. A stand still in negotiation.

**Lowballing.** The practice of giving a deceptively low price or cost estimate of a case in controversy. Sometimes called a boggy.

**Monologue in duet.** When individuals let their emotions rule their words and actions, resulting in a failure to express themselves clearly. Also, not listening to each other.

**Negotiate.** To deal with (some matter or affair that requires ability for its successful handling) or to arrange for or bring about through conference, discussion, and compromise. Working side by side to achieve mutually beneficial solutions.

**Neuro-linguistic programming.** A model of communication that assesses an individual's internal response mechanism that reacts to an external action, that ultimately forms an individual's response to a given situation.

**Objective criteria.** Any fair standards, independent of the desires of either side, which set the stage for impartial negotiations.

Looking at standards that exist in the marketplace independent of the pending transaction.

**Parrying.** To ward off (as a blow) or to evade especially by an adroit answer (*parry* an embarrassing question).

**Peacemaker.** A person who attempts to get everyone's perceptions aligned while trying to help people understand one another.

**Posturing.** To assume a posture; *especially* to strike a pose for effect or to assume an artificial or pretended attitude, i.e., a negotiator who acts indifferent, impatient, or condescending.

**Red herring.** A negotiation tactic based on a highly emotional issue that has no real substance to it used to create a time deficiency.

**Silence in negotiation.** A tactic that allows a skilled negotiator to keep their counterpart revealing information and making concessions.

**Smoke screen.** Anything that clouds the real issues at stake in a negotiation.

**Stalemate.** A drawn contest, deadlock. No movement in negotiation issues.

**Tactic.** A device for accomplishing an end. One of the many techniques used to get concessions in positional negotiations.

**Unsolicited information.** Unrequested information. Usually used to create diversion or misdirection in negotiation.